Hoover Institution Studies 35

Race and Politics
in Urban Malaya

Race and Politics
in Urban Malaya

Alvin Rabushka

Hoover Institution Press
Stanford, University
Stanford, California

The Hoover Institution on War, Revolution and Peace, founded at Stanford University in 1919 by the late President Herbert Hoover, is a center for advanced study and research on public and international affairs in the twentieth century. The views expressed in its publications are entirely those of the authors and do not necessarily reflect the views of the staff, officers, or Board of Overseers of the Hoover Institution.

Hoover Institution Studies 35
International Standard Book Number 0-8179-3351-4
Library of Congress Card Number 72-91040
© 1973 by the Board of Trustees of the
  Leland Stanford Junior University
All rights reserved
Printed in the United States of America

To My Parents

Contents

Tables

Acknowledgments

I accord special thanks to John D. Sprague for his assistance in formulating the research topic and for his help with the preliminary analysis of my sample survey of urban Malayans. Careful readings of various drafts of the manuscript and helpful comments were given by C. Paul Bradley, Cynthia H. Enloe, Roger Freeman, Lewis H. Gann, R. S. Milne, Rene Peritz, Marvin L. Rogers, Martin Rudner, Kenneth A. Shepsle, and Peter Wicks. For assistance during the various phases of two research trips to Malaya I want to thank Ramesh Chander, the Chief Statistician, the Registrar of Marriages, the Registrar of Societies, officials of the city councils of Kuala Lumpur and George Town (Penang), and many others in both private and public life who gave me their time. Grateful thanks are also given those who are the chief subjects of this book—the participants in a pioneer survey of racial and political attitudes.

For enduring the typing of several drafts of the manuscript, my thanks to Louise Doying. For editorial assistance I thank Barbara Pronin. The Hoover Institution on War, Revolution and Peace of Stanford University financed a second research trip to Malaya and the writing of the manuscript by providing a year's leave from teaching duties. The survey was previously financed in 1967 by the National Science Foundation and an NDEA-related Fulbright–Hays Award.

Again, I wish to acknowledge the help of all these people, who are, of course, not responsible for any errors of fact or interpretation this book may contain. That is my responsibility.

Race and Politics
in Urban Malaya

— 1 —

Introduction

No study of Malayan politics can omit a consideration of the most visible feature of Malayan society, namely, its multiracial population.* To the best of my knowledge, no recently published article or book on the subject makes such an omission, and this book is no different. Race is the dominant theme in this analysis of Malayan politics as well.

Unlike most standard historical narratives of Malayan politics, however, this book does not describe the overall workings of the political process or explain the how and why of current policies. It does not investigate the recruitment of elites for governing positions, their backgrounds, their political preferences, or their policy-making decisions. It does not analyze the constitution or the structures of government in great detail or ask whether the institutions provided for in the constitution are practical in Malaya's multiracial environment. Finally, it

* Malaya refers to the eleven peninsular states that make up West Malaysia, formerly known as the Federation of Malaya. Since I do not comment on events or personalities in the Borneo states of East Malaysia, the simpler term Malaya is used throughout—a common practice in studies of Malaysian politics. All residents of Malaya are called Malayans. The terms Malay, Chinese, and Indian refer to specific racial groups; the term Malayan, on the other hand, refers to any resident of Malaya, whatever his race. Writers about Malaya more often use the term "racial" rather than "ethnic," a usage reflecting the fact that all Malayans prefer to call their country multiracial rather than multiethnic.

does not offer detailed solutions to the problem of "democratic instability." [1]

What, then, does this book encompass, and how does it differ from other studies of Malayan politics? First, it examines the values, attitudes, and social and political behavior of the man in the street instead of reporting on dominant bureaucratic or elected political personalities, their parties, their electioneering, or their ultimate influence on the decisions of government. An analysis of the average citizen in the multiracial society may be as informative as the study of that society's elites, parties, and institutions, especially when information about racial values has hitherto been difficult to obtain. In many ways the beliefs of a citizenry limit the options open to decision makers; they circumscribe political alternatives and suggest the levels of popular support that leaders can expect for specific policies.

In addition, the setting of this book is limited to two cities: Kuala Lumpur, the federal capital and Malaya's most populous city, and George Town (hereafter Penang) on the Island of Penang, Malaya's second most populous and other major city. Rural Malaya is not included. How these two urban populations view the racial question, both in and out of a political context, is the focus of this book. Such information would be commonplace in a country whose candidates for elective office make frequent use of public opinion polls. But the survey I completed for this book in early 1967 is, to my knowledge, the first Gallup-type general public opinion poll ever conducted in Malaya on matters of race and politics, and I therefore hope to offer a more systematic treatment of interracial attitudes and interaction than has been published before.*

* Subsequent surveys of secondary and university school students on topics of race and politics were carried out in 1970 and 1971 by John Bock; see his forthcoming book *The Educational Correlates of Violence: A Case Study of Malaysia*. While Bock's surveys are geographically more representative of the nation than the present limited two-city sample, their respondents are far more restrictive by age, being composed entirely of young students or recent school graduates or

The specifically political data in this book are also restricted to Kuala Lumpur and Penang. My intention is to examine how the racial values and personal interactions of the respondents fit the politics of these two cities at the levels of local urban politics, state politics (for the Kuala Lumpur and Penang constituencies of the two respective state legislative assemblies), and national parliamentary politics (for the same constituencies). Data obtained in the survey are analyzed in conjunction with legal documents and election results to produce a vivid picture of urban politics. Of special interest is the relationship between the attitudes and corresponding political behavior of the different races. Thus, this book also features an intensive exploration of the city, a microcosm of Malayan multiracialism at its most sophisticated.*

The remainder of the first chapter describes the research procedures used in this book and concludes with a brief review of other work on the general subject of politics in multiracial societies, its forms, outcomes, and prospects. Chapter 2 provides a cultural and political setting for the book, accounts for the creation of a "plural society" in Malaya, describes that society in social, economic, and political terms, and, finally, presents the salient features of Kuala Lumpur and Penang. Chapter 3 offers a theoretical overview of Malayan politics as a background for the analysis of racial values and social behavior of the respondents (chapter 4) and their political behavior (chapter 5). The concluding chapter reviews the major findings and their implications.

leavers. What is important from a methodological point of view is that Bock was able to reinterview the same individuals over time and can thereby attest to the reliability of response on the sensitive topics of politics and race.

* Approximately 28.7 percent of all Malayans lived in urban areas in 1970. The figures for 1957 and 1947 were 26.5 percent and 15.9 percent respectively. Thus, the spread of urbanization suggests that the cities may become increasingly important in Malayan political life; see Malaysia. Chander, R., *1970 Population and Housing Census of Malaysia, Community Groups* (Kuala Lumpur: Department of Statistics, 1972), table XVI, p. 33.

RESEARCH PROCEDURES

Public opinion polls on questions of race, candidates for elective office, presidential popularity, and popular support for overseas wars are commonplace in the United States and on other appropriate topics in England, France, Northern Ireland, and India. That they are almost unheard of in Southeast Asia and in Malaya specifically was recognized very early by K. J. Ratnam in his seminal work *Communalism and the Political Process in Malaya.*

> Many of the observations found in this book, particularly those pertaining to communal attitudes, are in the main projections of expressed *elite* opinions . . . newspaper comments and so on, and are no doubt also influenced by my own familiarity with the Malayan political scene and participation in that society. . . .
>
> In the *absence of any extensive and carefully planned surveys,* it would be impossible to make claims about the accuracy of statements on communal attitudes. It may, of course, be possible roughly to estimate the relative popularity of different viewpoints on the basis of support given to different political parties whose chief distinguishing feature is their stand on the communal problem. But then the fortunes of these parties, because they are also influenced by other, often temporary, factors can easily fluctuate without corresponding fluctuations in the popular appreciation of their respective platforms. It is also relevant that leaders often succeed in "creating" the interests which they eventually seem to represent, a fact which limits the scope for generalizations on basic communal attitudes. *It may of course also be argued that, given the existence of political propaganda, even opinion surveys are liable to the same limitations* [italics mine]. [2]

Ratnam's observations are important on two counts. First, he notes the complete absence of surveys on communal attitudes in Malaya. Secondly, he raises the even more serious research question of what to make of, and how to evaluate, opinion surveys.

The usefulness and reliability of public opinion surveys in multiracial Malaya remains a serious concern for students of communalism and its underlying attitudes. In a later book coauthored with Professor R. S. Milne, Ratnam elaborates.

> In some developing countries public opinion polls have thrown some light on voting behavior. But it was not possible to arrange for any polls to be taken at the time of the 1964 general election in Malaya. Selection and training of interviewers and translation of questionnaires and replies (in at least four languages) would have been particularly formidable obstacles. Also, *any questions on opinions might not have been answered "honestly"* [italics mine]. If an interviewer were identified with the Government, the answers might have been deliberately deferential to the Government; if he were not so identified, no answer might have been forthcoming. Even if there had been no problem of finance, the polling operation would have required so much supervision and control that the authors would have been unduly distracted from the main course of the election study.[3]

Ratman and Milne are not alone in recognizing the absence of quantifiable, systematic information on communal values. Sociologist Gayl Ness quite correctly points this out in *Bureaucracy and Rural Development in Malaysia*.

> It is impossible to say with any precision and to what extent, or whether or not, the Malayan society is becoming less plural and more national in its basic groupings. There are essentially *no* data on Malayan values that would admit of even an educated guess on the degree of national consciousness that exists on any issue. *There are no studies of voting, opinions, or attitudes* on which the assessment of consensus might be made [italics mine].[4]

Ness not only recognizes that little is known about Malayan values; in the preface to his study he also questions the validity of information obtained by survey research procedures.

> I attempted to develop a survey instrument that could be applied systematically, but abandoned the efforts. In general I found it necessary to apply an evaluation of what was being said in an interview, and I could work out no suitable method of applying such an evaluation to a survey instrument. Especially in an interview that stretches over more than an hour, and then continues over a "stengah" at the rest house or over cocktails at a party, people contradict themselves directly and indirectly, often more than once on the same subject. It is not that they lie or deliberately attempt to deceive the questioner, though this does happen. It is merely a reflection of the great human capacity for holding conflicting ideas with little strain. The survey instrument normally achieves something like a snapshot of ideas, sentiments, and knowledge. I found it more useful to attempt to gain a life-like, moving version of the same phenomenon.[5]

Others, too, have noted the absence of extensive surveys on communal values or voting behavior. In a review of the Ratnam and Milne work, Robert O. Tilman, long a student of Malayan politics and bureaucracy, also expresses skepticism on the possibility of obtaining reliable survey data in Malaya.

> The American-trained political scientist of a more behavioral orientation is likely to find this book somewhat frustrating. Surely, he might conclude, the authors could have gotten more mileage out of their data. Indeed, I must admit some sympathy for this point of view, but I am also well aware of the restraints imposed on the authors by the very nature of their data. Even if they had preferred a more sophisticated and analytical approach, it is difficult to see how this might have been possible with the data available to them. Malaysian electoral districts, for the most part, do not coincide with the 1957 census districts, and thus correlations between

voting behavior and socio-economic variables are impossible. Moreover, to make it more difficult, the Malaysian government, for reasons best known to itself, chose not to release individual polling station voting statistics, and thus it is virtually impossible to manipulate census data to achieve even an educated guess about the impact of socio-economic variables. *Finally, public opinion polls and other forms of survey research are almost non-existent in Malaysia, and thus another door is closed in the face of the ambitious social scientist trained in the techniques of modern voting analysis* [italics mine].[6]

Tilman's assertions are more far-reaching than those of either Ratnam and Milne or Ness and, if correct, severely limit the scope of research on Malayan politics.* While he is quite correct in claiming that public opinion polls on politics or communal questions are almost nonexistent in Malaya, it does not follow that the techniques of modern survey research are not available to the "ambitious" social scientist.** Evidence, in fact, suggests the contrary.

In the early 1960s only one or two market research firms were in business in Malaya, among them Survey Research Malaysia, a worldwide Gallup affiliate, which began its Malaysian operations in 1964. By 1972 some nine distinct firms were engaged in market research, testifying to both the demand for its products and to its feasibility as well. In the area of consumer interest in new products, the survey research business has waxed and prospered. The remaining aspect of

---

* Ness, too, is sympathetic with Tilman's view. In discussing the relationship of education to values in his study of rural development, he cautions, "Unfortunately there are no studies of the impact of education on national consensus, and given the current sensitivity over 'communal issues' *it is doubtful that any such studies will be made in the near future.*" [italics mine]. Ness, *Bureaucracy and Rural Development in Malaysia,* p. 69.

** See Alvin Rabushka, "A Note on Overseas Chinese Political Participation in Urban Malaya," *American Political Science Review* 64, no. 1 (March 1970):177–78.

this controversy, then, involves the reliability and validity of specifically racial or political content surveys, and this aspect is admittedly more problematic. However, the results of Bock's more recent surveys on racial and political attitudes, coupled with the rapid growth of market research activity in Malaya, suggests that survey research on political or racial topics is not impossible at all.*

Questions of sensitivity in delicate political contexts have not deterred survey research in other plural societies. A good illustration is provided by Richard Rose, whose *Governing Without Consent: An Irish Perspective* reports the results of a survey of some two thousand respondents on the religious question in Northern Ireland.[7] Strictly speaking, it may be impossible ever to fully establish the validity of a survey, but procedures do exist that, if properly used, can minimize errors.

Tilman's review also raises the problem of the "ecological fallacy"—i.e., the fact that the way an individual votes cannot be directly obtained from an analysis of aggregate voting results. This problem will be considered in chapter 5, which contains an analysis of voting records for Kuala Lumpur and Penang.

The Survey

The Kuala Lumpur and Penang interviews were completed by Survey Research Malaysia, an independent public opinion and market research firm, whose staff, at the time of the survey, had divided the major towns in Malaya into Enumeration Areas (or blocks) on a geographical basis. One-fifth of the blocks were selected at random and fully houselisted. Households were serially identified, and location maps were drawn to supplement each block houselisting.

* Although polls can reveal underlying values and normal social and political behavior, they are less useful in telling us how groups of individuals will react in crisis situations.

A random sample was established of 500 households each in Kuala Lumpur and Penang. These households were expected to yield over 350 adults in each city by selecting for interview one adult in every 3.5 listed as described below. In each city, twenty-four blocks were selected using random number tables. A large number of blocks was used to ensure a wide spread and to avoid emphasis on any single characteristic (such as ethnicity or social class) that tends to be geographically concentrated. In each block, households were selected from a random starting point—at every twelfth interval in Kuala Lumpur and every sixth in Penang. This procedure permits conclusions to be drawn independently for Kuala Lumpur and Penang but does not allow the possibility of any meaningful totaling of the two without the application of weighting factors. The sample is self-weighting within each city.

At each household the interviewer listed all persons aged fifteen or older in descending order of age. He was instructed to number these adults serially and to check the numbering against a series of qualifying numbers. Interviews were conducted only with the adult or adults selected for interview by this method. This system of adult selection gives appropriate representation to all individuals, irrespective of the size of their household.

The interviewer was told to interview only those selected for interview, even if this meant making an appointment to return. In case of difficulty, two additional attempts were made to contact the selected adult. No substitution within a household was allowed, and the interviewer was allowed no discretion in the selection of households. In the event of noncontact (house not located or refusal to participate), the next address on the contact sheet was substituted.

Application of the respective sampling fractions gave 538 households in Kuala Lumpur and 500 in Penang. Interviews were conducted in 352 households in Kuala Lumpur and 307 in Penang. Some of the reasons for noninterview included vacant address (30 in Kuala Lumpur, 14 in Penang), household refusals (12 and 30), inability to locate (14 and 16), houses demolished (2 and 3), households not attempted (0 and 27), and no qualifying adult (93 and 87). Of the 538 households selected in Kuala Lumpur and the 500 in Penang, a total of 186 and 193 respectively did not participate in the survey. The primary reason for noninterview was the unavailability of the selected adult after three visits. *Only 3 persons in Kuala Lumpur and 2 in Penang refused to allow an interview within the selected households.*

Field work began in Kuala Lumpur on 16 February 1967 and ended on 27 February 1967; field work began in Penang on 22 February 1967 and ended on 7 March 1967. Since the two periods overlapped, systematic differences that might be attributable to disturbing society-wide variables or events during the two periods were reasonably well controlled. Although interviewers encountered some resistance to questions on political issues, there was virtually no resistance to questions about race. The questionnaire was translated into Malay, Chinese, and Tamil and administered in either English, Malay, Tamil, or an appropriate Chinese dialect by interviewers of these races (the English questionnaire is included in Appendix 1).

This survey provided the first opportunity to explore the racial values and political behavior of a representative sample of urban Malayan individuals. It is precisely these types of data that professors Ness and Ratnam insist are vital but that had heretofore been unavailable.

Nonsurvey Data

To augment the information collected directly from individuals during the survey, I also examined a variety of other source materials in three categories: (1) legal documentation, (2) election results and other published statistics, and (3) the works of other specialists. Legal documentation includes all constitutional and other legal enactments that apply to local, state, or national politics in Kuala Lumpur or Penang. These documents define the political rules and changes in those rules and may thus be viewed as the formal outcomes of public decisions. A chronological review of the changes in law abundantly reveals the problems that racially distinct urban concentrations pose for democratic governments when the urban masses differ racially from the national ruling race.

The reports published by the Election Commission indicate the vote totals for each electoral contest by constituency; they list the candidates, their party affiliations, and votes obtained, and other pertinent information, such as the number of spoiled ballots. They are invariably prefaced by a description of the tasks involved in preparing for the election, an analysis of the turnout, and some conjecture on the meaning of the results for the country. Other useful information is to be found in the census reports and publications of the Statistics Department and other branches of government.

To gain additional background and insight into these election returns and legal changes, I interviewed a number of prominent Malayan citizens both in and out of government. While I do not report these valuable interviews in detail,* I have tried to confirm the useful facts uncovered by checking relevant documentation or statistics. That which could not be independently verified is not presented.**

---

* My analysis of political outcomes and changes is the result of an examination of historical legal documents and a quantitative analysis of election results. It does not depend on confidential, off-the-record comments by knowledgeable informants, whose understanding of Malayan politics may either be biased, limited, or plain wrong, both factually and in matters of interpretation.

** It is easy to succumb to the rumor mongering that arises when interviewing important people. While such 'informants' can gossip and speculate, they do not (often cannot) tell you what the mass of voters think on any given issue. Their familiarity with the political scene is often helpful and perceptive, but it is not necessarily accurate.

Already published studies of Malayan politics and society provide a third and copious source of useful material on communalism and racial politics. The interested reader is referred to the Bibliography in which some of that material is listed.

A VIEW OF PLURAL SOCIETY *

Most students term Malaya a "plural society." [8] The term was first introduced by J. S. Furnivall in *Netherlands India,* in which he defined a plural society as "comprising two or more elements or social orders which live side by side, yet without mingling, in one political unit." [9] Its distinguishing features include: (1) the fact that rulers and ruled are of different races and live apart from one another in separate communities; (2) the absence of a national consensus—i.e., a set of cultural and political values shared by the different communities; (3) the coincidence of economic activities with racial divisions— i.e., the tendency to cast economic conflict in racial terms; (4) the reliance on the marketplace as the only common meeting ground for the different races; and (5) the assertion that plural societies are inherently prone to conflict and therefore require some external force to hold them together, a prime candidate being colonial rule.

The latter point has been, and still is, controversial. Put simply, Furnivall suggests that persons of different races are not likely to coexist peacefully unless a strong government keeps them away from each other. Time, shared experiences, antidiscriminatory legislation, guarantees of civil rights and/or education do not ensure that separate communities can learn to live together peacefully. The assertion carries strong prescriptive overtones—namely, that the granting of

---

* A review of the conceptual and theoretical treatments given to "plural societies" can be found in Alvin Rabushka and Kenneth A. Shepsle, *Politics in Plural Societies,* chap. 1. The major parts of that discussion are summarized in the following paragraphs.

independence to colonial plural societies, however well designed or intended, may be unwarranted and very risky.

These implications have been challenged by many scholars
who argue that factionalism within communal groups, mutual
understanding of cultural values and activities of other
groups, and the development of multiracial class movements
would enable citizens of a plural society to live together
peacefully under democratic governments.[10] Others have
sought partial modifications of Furnivall's conflict framework
or have tried to combine aspects of both the conflict and consensus schools.[11] Explicitly political analyses of the multiracial society have also been made under the rubric of political
integration and have resulted in a substantial body of literature.[12] There is, however, no agreement about the conditions
necessary and sufficient to maintain a peaceful, stable democracy in culturally diverse societies. We are left with a collage of
opinions and widespread disagreement on definitions, theories,
and concepts, as well as on what to make of available evidence.

The author's own view of the plural society concept has already been spelled out in detail.[13] The concept is used here,
and the intellectual background is provided for it, because it
captures the qualitative features of Malayan society so well.
Briefly, a plural society is identified by: (1) cultural diversity,
(2) the existence of politically organized cultural communities,
and (3) the overwhelming prominence of race in politics. While
this definition distinguishes plural societies from both homogeneous and more pluralistic societies in which race is not salient, it does not account for the distinction. It does, however,
enable us to classify Malaya as a plural society, with the result
that we are in a position to decide, on the basis of observation
and analysis, which of the prophecies about plural societies
seems most appropriate.

— 2 —

Cultural and Political Setting

Malaya lies just barely north of the equator, between 1° and 7° latitude North, and is an intensely hot and humid country. Plants grow profusely—the papaya grows from a seedling to bear full-sized edible fruit in just seven months—and the cities, if left untended by man, would soon revert to jungle. For this reason, archaeology is not a rewarding enterprise in Malaya. What is known about prehistoric Malaya is based more on the travel records of surrounding countries than on archaeological excavation within the country itself.

Several delightful illustrations of this are found in the Chinese dynastic histories, which often reported the overseas adventures of prominent Chinese.[1] Even more revealing is the fact that the founding of the Malacca Sultanate, the first genuinely indigenous political kingdom (about A.D. 1400), is based more on legend than on hard historical documentation. The legend is that a rebellious prince in one of the neighboring Indonesian states maneuvered his way to the present port of Malacca and established his sultanate at the crossroads of the Malacca Straits, then as now a vital international waterway. He embraced Islam and became prosperous, and his kingdom provided the model for the present-day Malay Sultanate.

Though the Malays arrived and established their position far in advance of other immigrant communities, three distinct categories of aborigines, who long predate the Malays, were

16

the original inhabitants of the peninsula.[2] Their numbers are diminishing today, not because of ill treatment, but because those who intermarry with Malays and become Muslims become absorbed into the Malay community. The aborigines, however, are politically unimportant and play no role in this book.

The Malays, who give the country its name, are believed to have originated in the Indonesian islands, particularly Sumatra. Although trading contacts were established with Hindu India and Confucian China as early as the seventh century B.C., few non-Malays took up permanent residence. Before the arrival of the Europeans in 1509, Malayans were racially homogeneous. Most regarded themselves as Malays, spoke the Malay language, practiced Islam, and adhered to Malay custom and ritual.[3]

This condition persisted under the Portuguese, who seized Malacca by force in 1511, the Dutch, who captured it in 1641, and under the early stages of British rule. The British acquired Penang from the Sultan of Kedah in 1786 and added Malacca to it in 1795. When the Anglo-Dutch treaty of 1824 once and for all fixed British authority over the former Dutch-ruled Malayan territories, Malaya was still racially homogenous.

The changing racial composition of Malaya may be attributed to several causes, chiefly British immigration policy. The British, who adhered to the laissez-faire policy of free movement of labor and capital, accepted and even encouraged Chinese immigration. The Chinese were eager to move to Malaya to pursue their own economic self-interest.

British economic policy—enforcement of private property rights, maintenance of law and order, and minimum interference in the cultural affairs of individuals—together with the virtual breakdown of law and order in South China during and after the Taiping Rebellion (1850–64) brought substantial Chinese immigration into the Straits Settlements of Penang, Malacca, and Singapore. Had China been prosperous and well governed, as she was at the start of the Ch'ing Dynasty in the middle and late 1600s, Malaya might never have become economically attractive to the Chinese.

Critics with the benefit of hindsight often blame the British for not bringing the Chinese into the mainstream of Malayan cultural, social, and political life and for allowing them to maintain a separate and transient outlook. This criticism is true and helps to explain why the Chinese retain their own traditions in modern Malaya, but it disregards the British policy of allowing an individual the right to practice his own culture. Had the British tried forcibly to weld the Chinese into a Malayan nation, historians might have accused them of cultural genocide. Substantial British interference in Chinese cultural affairs would, in any case, have curtailed the inflow of Chinese and thereby disrupted the laissez-faire policy. One last point on the subject of Chinese immigration: though the bulk of early Chinese immigrants settled in the British-ruled Straits Settlements, a substantial number came in response to Malay recruiters. The Malay sultans themselves acquired Chinese workers to help in their tin enterprises.

Indians comprise the third major element in Malaya's cultural mosaic. It may be that miserable conditions in India, especially in the Tamil state of Madras, gave rise to a large outflow of Tamils seeking work abroad. Tamils compose important communities today in such remote places as Mauritius, Trinidad, Guyana, Fiji, and Ceylon. Why? Because the British found the Tamil to be a capable plantation worker, whether growing sugar, picking tea leaves, or, as in Malaya, tapping rubber. The successful introduction of the rubber seedling into Singapore's Botanic Gardens required a large supply of cheap labor. Tamils filled the bill. Just over 80 percent of the Indians in Malaya trace their origins to Madras; the rest came as merchants, professionals, and as nonstate agricultural workers (e.g., to raise dairy herds). Indian immigration was due almost entirely to the pressures and incentives of the colonial planters. They were not invited by, or readily accepted into, the Malay community.

There is still a small but economically important foreign community in Malaya, whose members for the most part reflect the historical importance of the colonial commercial experience; the import-export houses, the banks, the tin mines, and the major rubber estates are mostly British-owned and operated. European commercial interests were felt in public policy until 1957 (the date of Malayan independence) and for some years after that. Martin Rudner concludes that estate owners remained influential even after independence; he shows that the policies of the Alliance government "effectively sacrificed smallholders' greater needs to the canons of conservative finance," thereby working to the advantage of the large European-owned estates.[4]

The picture is now relatively complete. Malays, who make up the largest community, claim to be the original inhabitants, and therefore the rightful owners, of the land. They view the Chinese and Indians as more or less permanent guests originally brought in as transients by the tin and plantation interests. The Europeans no longer dictate policy but still play an important economic role. Foreigners, for instance, own 62.1 percent of the assets of the limited companies that engage in commercial and industrial activities, in contrast with 22.8 percent for Chinese, 1.5 percent for Malays, and 0.9 percent for Indians.[5]

THE PLURAL SOCIETY IN MALAYA: A DESCRIPTION

The dominant features of Furnivall's plural society include residentially separated communities, economic differentiation by race, uneven distributions of wealth, little intermarriage, and most important, one politically dominant community. Does this description fit Malaya?

Racial distributions in Malaya have remained relatively constant over the last half-century. Table 1 shows that the Malays have hovered near the 50 percent mark in every census taken since 1931, with a dramatic upward shift in the last five years. That Malays in 1970 comprise over half the population calms Malay fears that higher Chinese and Indian fertility would convert them into a permanent minority.* Urbanization has apparently held down the size of Chinese families, and this trend is expected to continue.**

Residential patterns of segregation are easily identifiable but somewhat complex. There are two major sets of distinctions. First, the East Coast of the peninsula is predominantly Malay in comparison to the much more multiracial West Coast. Secondly, throughout the eleven Malay states, Chinese are concentrated in urban areas, whereas Malays are chiefly rural. The East Coast traveler sees few Chinese outside the towns of Kota Bahru and Kuala Trengganu. The West Coast traveler, on the other hand, is impressed by the Chinese flavor of the cities; Chinese and English are heard more often than Malay. Along the West Coast, many Chinese practice commercial agriculture.

Few immigrants inhabit Kelantan and Trengganu, the two most traditional East Coast Malay states (see Table 2). The few Chinese found in these states tend to live in the towns, thus giving the rural areas an exclusive Malay coloration. On the other hand, Penang, Perak, Negri Sembilan, Selangor,

---

* This fear is neither unfounded nor trivial. Higher East Indian birth rates have made the Fijians and Guyanese Africans a permanent minority in their nations.

** In Table XVI, p. 33 of the *1970 Population and Housing Census of Malaysia, Community Groups,* the urban/rural patterns by race are displayed for 1947, 1957, and 1970. The Malay proportion of the population now living in urban areas has grown from 11.2 percent in 1957 to 14.9 in 1970; the Chinese from 44.7 to 47.4; and the Indians from 30.6 to 34.7. Thus, on balance, Indians and Chinese are far more heavily urbanized than Malays. This may account for the more rapid increase in Malay population.

Table 1

RACIAL COMPOSITION OF MALAYA'S POPULATION
FROM 1921 TO 1970 BY PERCENTAGES

Racial Group	*(N=2,907,000)* 1921	*(N=3,788,000)* 1931	*(N=4,908,000)* 1947	*(N=6,279,000)* 1957	*(N=8,039,000)* 1965	*(N=8,810,348)* 1970
Malays	54.0	49.2	49.5	49.8	50.1	53.2
Chinese	29.4	33.9	38.4	37.2	36.8	35.4
Indians	15.1	15.1	10.8	11.3	11.1	10.6
Others	1.5	1.8	1.3	1.8	2.0	0.8

Sources: 1957 Population Census, Report No. 14, adapted from Table 1.3, p. 3; estimates from Monthly Statistical Bulletin of the States of Malaya, September 1966; and 1970 Population and Housing Census of Malaysia, Community Groups, Table VI, p. 27.

Table 2   RACIAL COMPOSITION BY STATE
                 BY PERCENTAGES, 1970

State	Malays	Chinese	Indians
Trengganu (405,539) *	93.9	5.4	0.6
Kelantan (686,266)	92.8	5.3	0.8
Perlis (120,991)	79.4	16.2	2.0
Kedah (954,749)	70.7	19.3	8.4
Pahang (504,900)	61.2	31.2	7.3
Malacca (404,135)	51.8	39.6	7.8
Johore (1,276,969)	53.4	39.4	6.7
Negri Sembilan (481,491)	45.4	38.1	16.1
Perak (1,569,161)	43.1	42.5	14.2
Penang ** (775,440)	30.7	56.1	11.5
Selangor ** (1,630,707)	34.6	46.3	18.3

Source: *1970 Population and Housing Census of Malaysia, Commu-
          nity Groups,* Table XIV, p. 32, and Table 1, p. 45.

Notes: * The numbers in parentheses indicate the population of the
          state. The percentages are read horizontally as proportions of
          the total state population comprised by each ethnic group.
          ** The States of Penang and Selangor contain, respectively,
          the cities of George Town and Kuala Lumpur, the sites of the
          field research.

Malacca, and Johore—the modern West Coast states—are
heavily populated by immigrants. In the first four of these
states Malays are a minority.

The cities are the more economically advanced sector of
the Malayan economy, and their domination by the immigrant races is even more pronounced. Table 3 indicates that
Chinese make up nearly 60 percent of all urban dwellers; Malays, close to two-thirds of all rural inhabitants. Thus, it is
easy to meet Furnivall's first qualification—residential segregation by race. The few existing multiracial neighborhoods do
not distort the overall pattern of racial concentration and separation.

Economic differentiation by race—the second feature—is
equally easy to establish. Malays, by and large, are found in

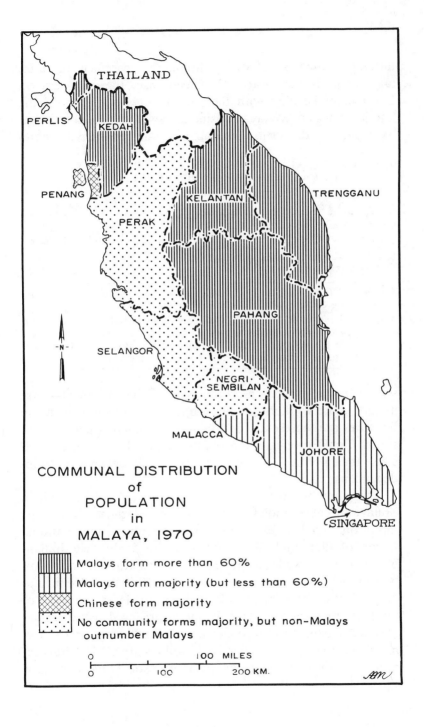

THAILAND

PERLIS

KEDAH

PENANG

PERAK

KELANTAN

TRENGGANU

PAHANG

SELANGOR

NEGRI
SEMBILAN

MALACCA

JOHORE

SINGAPORE

COMMUNAL DISTRIBUTION
of
POPULATION
in
MALAYA, 1970

Malays form more than 60%

Malays form majority (but less than 60%)

Chinese form majority

No community forms majority, but non-Malays
outnumber Malays

0   100 MILES

0   100   200 KM.

farming, fishing, small rubber holdings, the police, the military, and, as has historically been true, the civil service. Chinese, in keeping with their urban life style, control the middle sectors of Malayan business; they dominate commerce, banking, and domestic manufacturing and are heavily repre-

Table 3   RACIAL COMPOSITION OF URBAN AND
RURAL POPULATION BY PERCENTAGES

Type of Area	Malays	Chinese	Indians
Urban—10,000 population + (N = 2,530,433) (28.7%)	27.6	58.5	12.8
Rural—less than 10,000 population (N = 6,279,915) (71.3%)	63.5	26.2	9.7

Source: 1970 Population and Housing Census of Malaysia, Community Groups, adapted from Table XI, p. 30.

Note: The proportions are read from left to right. For example, 27.6 percent of the urban residents are Malays, 58.5 percent are Chinese, and 12.8 percent are Indians. Altogether, 28.7 percent of the population live in urban areas.

sented in the professions. Indians, as Table 4 indicates, are mainly estate workers (rubber tappers), but those who live in the cities are represented in Malaya's commercial and professional life. (Europeans are omitted from this discussion because their political importance has steadily declined since independence.)

Trade unions have not played an important political role in Malaya because Indians have dominated them since their inception. The largest union in the country, the National Union of Plantation Workers, is almost exclusively Indian-based. Indians made up 58 percent of all trade union members in 1957, increased to 62 percent in 1960, and declined to 48 percent in 1964.[6] But as Indians are the least numerous of the three races in Malaya, it is not surprising that the nationalist movement developed outside of the trade union movement. Several of the earlier trade unions—e.g., General Laborer's Union, Pan-Malayan Federation of Trade Unions—

Table 4 ECONOMICALLY ACTIVE POPULATION
PERCENTAGES BY RACIAL GROUP
AND OCCUPATION, 1957

Industry	(N = 1,023,729) Malays	(N = 771,963) Chinese	(N = 312,956) Indians
Agriculture, Forestry, Hunting, and Fishing	45.0	13.1	1.4
Estate Agriculture	28.2	27.2	54.3
Mining and Quarrying	1.0	5.2	2.2
Manufacturing	2.6	12.6	3.5
Building and Construction	2.2	4.2	3.9
Electricity, Gas, and Water	0.4	0.4	1.3
Commerce	3.1	16.5	10.4
Transportation, Storage, and Communication	2.6	3.8	5.1
Services	12.5	14.2	15.4
Unspecified or Inadequately Described	0.6	1.2	0.8
Unemployed but Looking for Work	1.9	1.7	1.8

Source: 1957 Population Census, Report No. 14, adapted from Table
No. 12, pp. 111–22.

were Chinese-led, well organized, militant, and politically
conscious. But postwar colonial rule eliminated most of the
militant political elements from trade unionism; thereafter it
was dominated by the more passive Indian community. On
the whole, the trade union movement in Malaya has been
more of a nuisance than a support to the Malay government.[7]

Economic specialization by race helps to explain the
marked disparities in per capita income. An Inland Revenue

Department survey of household budgets in 1958 arrived at the following annual estimates: Malays—M$359, Chinese—M$848, and Indian—M$691.* On a national scale, Malays earn approximately 30 percent of total income, Chinese, 54 percent, and Indians, 13 percent.[8] Although each race has its rich and poor, the overall picture is one of Chinese affluence and Malay poverty.

Malays, Chinese, and Indians are thus segregated by state, city, occupation, and wealth, and there are cultural distinctions between them as well. Malays speak a distinct language (Malay), practice Islam (which is not optional but required by the constitution), and maintain unique customs and practices. Chinese speak a number of Chinese dialects, may practice Buddhism, Confucianism, Taoism, or Christianity, and maintain their own customs and practices, some of which—specifically the strong taste for pork (ritually proscribed for Malays) and the penchant for gambling—are extremely annoying to Malays. Finally, Indians speak mainly Tamil or a variety of other Indian languages, profess Hinduism (a few are Muslims), and are easily identified by their styles of dress, eating, and other cultural traits. It is easy to identify the race of any given Malayan. Female dress, for example, immediately establishes race: sarongs for Malays, cheongsams and samfus for Chinese, and saris for Indians. Racial guessing is not difficult even when Western dress is worn, as gestures, accent, appearance, and choice of restaurant are often indicators. Malaya is an attractive field site for students of interracial interaction.

Not surprisingly, intermarriage is rare in Malaya, perhaps no more than one percent, in the past or the present.[9] The survey respondents and their parents establish exactly seven intermarriages (out of a total of more than 750); an analysis of marriage records in Kuala Lumpur and Penang confirms 23 of a total of 4,809 recorded in 1956, 1961, and 1966.

* M$3.00 approximately equals US$1.00.

Thus, Furnivall's definition of the plural society does fit Malaya, but our own definition (see chapter 1) of plural societies fits Malaya as well. To establish the existence in Malaya of politically organized cultural communities and their agents, the racial parties, requires the historical review of pre- and post-independence politics that follows.

A HISTORICAL BACKGROUND OF MALAYAN POLITICS

This section on the rules of Malayan politics does not offer a formal analysis of the constitution.[10] As will be seen, the constitution has been periodically adjusted to suit Malay interests as well as to enshrine Malay political supremacy. The paragraphs that follow review the historical events that have given rise to this condition.

The British acquired Penang in 1786 from the Sultan of Kedah in exchange for money and guarantees of military protection from the Thais. Although the British did not honor their pledge of military assistance, they nonetheless went on to acquire Malacca in 1795 and Singapore, which they established as a free port in 1819 under the governorship of Stamford Raffles. These three territories were jointly administered as the Straits Settlements, and their rule passed from the East India Company to the British crown in 1856. Henceforth, and until Malayan independence in 1957, the Straits Settlements were ruled as a direct colony of the crown, with their residents qualifying as British-protected subjects.

The British also expanded their influence into the Malayan hinterland, establishing a policy of "indirect rule" in the states of Perak, Selangor, Negri Sembilan, and Pahang. It should be emphasized that the British were unwilling imperialists in this entire affair. They refused several earlier requests and reluctantly intervened only when British firms in the Straits Settlements (concerned that fighting would disrupt the tin trade) buttressed a direct request from one of the three claimants to the Sultanate of Perak. The sultan indicated his willingness, if supported by the British, to accept a resident British adviser. The Perak chiefs ultimately chose the British-supported candidate, and a treaty was signed that provided for a British resident whose advice was to be respected and obeyed on all matters except Malay religion and custom. Law and order and revenues collection henceforth lay in British hands.

Indirect rule worked well on paper, but the resident of Perak did not know how to put it into practice and was murdered by outraged Malays. British troops avenged his death, and the lessons of British force were thoroughly understood by subsequent generations of Malays. Thereafter, the British grew steadily stronger while the autonomy and authority of the sultans increasingly diminished. The first visible sign of a deteriorating Malay position appeared in 1895 when the Federated Malay States came into being. Under this arrangement, each resident was responsible to the governor of the Straits Settlements, and in the interest of administrative uniformity every important department in the governments of the four states was put under a single administrative head.

Kedah, Perlis, Kelantan, Trengganu, and Johore—the five remaining Malay states—each ultimately accepted a resident adviser, but the five sultans, fearing a loss of prestige and autonomy, refused to join the Federated Malay States; they remained administratively distinct and were referred to as the "Unfederated Malay States." These administrative classifications—the Straits Settlements, the Federated Malay States, and the Unfederated Malay States—remained intact between the two world wars. All attempts to bring the five unfederated states into a broader federation failed.

Racial battle lines were being drawn in the 1930s over the issue of decentralization, a policy sought by some of the sultans and high-ranking colonial officers. Decentralization was, however, opposed by both European and Chinese business interests who feared that an increase in Malay political freedom would upset commerce and financial stability. Naturally, Chinese opposition to decentralization did not win them the affection of Malays. In addition, the Chinese were treated by colonial officials as "transients" rather than as permanent, coequal citizens of Malaya. Although decentralization should have been attractive to all the sultans, those of the unfederated states refused to join a broader decentralized federation, being suspicious and distrustful of further tamperings with their internal autonomy.

And for good reason. Immediate postwar colonial policy in the form of the Malayan Union threatened to destroy permanently the privileged position of the sultan and the protected status of the Malays. If implemented, the Malayan Union would have given Malayans of all races substantially equal citizenship rights and, even more disturbing, would have replaced the patchwork of the Straits Settlements, Federated Malay States, and Unfederated Malay States with a unitary state, setting Singapore off as a separate crown colony. The Malayan Union represented a radical break from the tradition of indirect rule and Malay supremacy.

A loud uproar accompanied the installation of Sir Edward Gent, the first British governor under the new Malayan Union.[11] Protest was not limited to the sultans and their supporters. Many retired British civil servants in London who had served in Malaya objected vigorously in the press and in high government circles as well. Meanwhile, under the urging of Dato Onn bin Ja'afar, the founder of the United Malays National Organization, the Malay rulers boycotted the installation of the new governor. The sustained and unified resistance of the Malay community led the Colonial Office to reconsider these constitutional arrangements, and the Malayan Union was replaced on 1 February 1948 with the Federation of Malaya, the settlement that would become the basis of the constitution of independent Malaya.

The new settlement reestablished Malay supremacy—as might be expected since the Chinese and Indians played almost no part in its drafting. On paper, Malaya was to have a parliamentary system combined with an elected constitutional monarchy, the king being chosen every five years from among the reigning sultans. The actual power lay not with the king, of course, but with parliament, the cabinet, and the prime minister's office. Although a federal form of government was specified, the central government saw its powers rise dramatically. As proof of this, the central government is now responsible for nearly 80 percent of total government expenditures in Malaya, the balance belonging to the states and local authorities.[12] A veto on any legislation affecting the rights, powers, and privileges of the sultans is retained by the sultans as specified in the constituion.

This brief historical review reveals that the political tradition in Malaya has regarded the Malays as privileged and protected, as the rightful owners of the land, and Indians and Chinese as "transients," second-class citizens preoccupied with making money. What does Malay supremacy entail? First, and crucial from the standpoint of electoral politics, it entails citizenship. All Malays immediately qualified for Malayan citizenship as subjects of their respective sultans, but not so the Chinese and Indians. Although the laws have been relaxed since 1957, citizenship was initially more difficult for non-Malays to obtain. The 1955 Legislative Council elections revealed how difficult—84 percent of the registered electorate was Malay. This imbalance has now mostly disappeared, but it served at the outset to ensure Malay electoral victory.

The language issue has also dominated Malayan politics for many years, especially with regard to education.[13] Unlike Singapore, where English, Malay, Chinese, and Tamil are all official languages (i.e., administrative languages of government), Malay alone is the national language of Malaya; since 1967 it has also been the sole official language. Language controversy has embattled the domestic politics of many multilingual peoples, Ceylon, Belgium, and Canada among them. Determined to avoid the Ceylon bloodbath, Tunku Abdul Rahman, prime minister of Malaya from 1957 to 1970, believed he was pursuing the correct policy by imposing Malay as the sole official language of the country. Right or wrong, the policy was distasteful to the Chinese community; on several occasions Chinese communal parties championed multilingualism on behalf of the Chinese electorate. This issue is now constitutionally proscribed, but it remains a serious concern for the Chinese, who fear the loss of their culture and ultimately the dissolution of Chinese schools. Although the constitution contains a clause presumably guaranteeing the legitimate rights of other communities, the Chinese have good reason to be dubious of constitutional guarantees. (The law has even been tampered with to eliminate local elections in which Chinese candidates have been disproportionately successful.)

The words "Malay Special Privileges" are extremely important in the Malayan political context and are the bane of non-Malays. Article 153 of the constitution provides: (1) the reservation for Malays of four-fifths of all appointments in the Malayan Civil Service, the most important branch of the public services; (2) the reservation for Malays of three-fourths of all university scholarships; and (3) the prerogative of the king to issue new permits or licenses as required by federal law to Malays in whatever proportion he deems reasonable. A fourth guarantee in Article 89 provides for a system of Malay reservations—land reserved for Malays that cannot be alienated into non-Malay hands. The land reservations include large tracts in the states and smaller tracts in the cities. Kampong Bahru, for example, is a section of Malay-reserved land in the heart of Kuala Lumpur, just north of the central business district. The taxation rates on this land are only one-fourth to one-half that levied on property elsewhere in the city, so that non-Malays, in effect, subsidize urban services for its residents.

Special privileges thus means a system of quotas in the public service, higher education (Malays now make up an increasingly larger proportion of university students than before), and in the issuing of new business licenses and permits. The Constitutional Commission recommended, though it was not stated formally in the constitution, that the matter of Malay special privileges be reviewed after fifteen years, but the severe rioting that followed the general elections in May 1969 led the government to announce that it would henceforth be unlawful for anyone to raise publicly the issue of Malay privileges. They are now, in short, a permanent feature of Malayan life.

Two other important provisions of the constitution merit emphasis—Articles 149 and 150, which permit such infringements on civil liberties as "preventive detention" when hostility between the races might arouse violence and "proclamations of emergency" which permits, among other things, the suspension of elections. Moreover, Article 10, which guarantees the rights of free speech, peaceful assembly, and of forming associations also provides that Parliament may restrict these rights for reasons of security or public order. Restrictions can also be imposed on the freedom of movement of politically suspect persons. In fact, the powers to restrict civil rights are so sweeping as to invalidate the guarantees of them. States of emergency have been in effect from 1948 to 1960, 1963 to 1966, and 1969 to 1971. Most of Malaya's post-independence history has transpired under states of emergency, and civil rights have often been disregarded. These restrictions on freedom undoubtedly distress the Chinese more than the Malays.

Indeed, the Chinese are entitled to their suspicions of constitutional guarantees. Table 3 indicates that the Malays are predominantly rural and the Chinese predominantly urban in their dwelling habits. Constitutional amendments normally require a two-thirds majority in both houses of Parliament, the Dewan Ra'ayat (house of representatives), and the Dewan Negara (the senate). Recalling that the early citizenship requirements produced a disproportionately large Malay electorate, it is easy to see why citizenship requirements have been steadily relaxed.

One explanation can be found in a specific constitutional amendment passed in 1962. This amendment, listed in the Thirteenth Schedule of the constitution, provides that

> the number of electors within each constituency ought to be approximately equal throughout the unit of review except that, having regard to the greater difficulty of reaching electors in the country districts and the other disadvantages facing rural constituencies, a measure of weightage for areas ought to be given to such constituencies, to the extent that in some cases *a rural constituency may contain as little as one half of the electors of any urban constituency* [italics mine].

Electoral arrangements favor the predominantly rural Malays through the smaller size of rural constituencies, so that Malays need not stuff the ballot box to retain control of Parliament; to all intents and purposes, a rural Malay is politically equivalent to two urban Chinese. Thus constitutional guarantees are effective only insofar as the politically dominant community respects the rights of minorities. The Malay community has used the constitution for its own interests, as confirmed by both the above illustration and the Malay refusal to accept the Malayan Union. Their precarious economic position vis-à-vis the Chinese has often been cited as a compelling reason for these measures.

An element of critical political importance not specified in the constitution is the racial composition of the military and police forces. Though exact percentages are lacking, the Chinese disdain police or army work. Consequently, with the exception of various technical and medical services, the army is mainly Malay and the same is true of the police. Malay dominance of the police and the army is a form of insurance in defense of their constitutional privileges and guarantees. Rule by decree, for example, as carried out from May 1969

until February 1971 when parliament was reinstated, is by
and large rule by Malay decree, even though an occasional
Malay extremist may be hurt.

An analysis of Malayan politics requires at least a rudi-
mentary acquaintance with the structure of the political
parties. Most analysts of parties in Malaya use the communal—noncommunal dichotomy in which parties are described as either multiracial in organization and composition
or exclusively racial in membership. It is notable that none
of the multiracial parties in Malaya has ever had sustained
electoral success. That they generally fail to survive in itself
testifies to the salience of race in Malayan politics. In de-
scribing these parties, it is essential not to confuse goals and
membership requirements with actual practices and policies.
What often appears on paper to be a noncommunal or multiracial party almost invariably turns out to be non-Malay,
predominately Chinese-based. Perhaps the best way to cate-
gorize the parties is, first, to distinguish between Malay and
non-Malay parties; secondly, to position them on the mod-
erate-extreme continuum on racial issues (their position on
economic issues is unimportant); and thirdly, to examine
the success or failure of both the multiracial and coalition-of-
races parties. The relatively unimportant National Association of Perak, the Malayan Party, and the National Conven-
tion Party are not discussed.[14]

The most important party in Malaya is the United Malays
National Organization (UMNO). Led in 1946 by Dato
Onn bin Ja'afar, it fought for and obtained a federation to
replace the unacceptable Malayan Union. But Dato Onn's
visions of a truly multiracial nationalist party were not enthusiastically received by the vast majority of party members.
Disappointed, he withdrew from UMNO and with some of his
followers founded the Independence of Malaya Party to put
his wish for multiracialism into practice. This party floundered in the Kuala Lumpur municipal elections of 1952, was
recast in 1954 as the Party Negara with a more pro-Malay

orientation, but again floundered in the 1955 Legislative Council elections. Dato Onn was even defeated in his own home constituency in Johore. Unfortunately for his career, he misread the mood of the electorate on the question of multiracial parties.

In August 1951 Tunku Abdul Rahman was installed as head of UMNO and remained in that position until 1971, when he gave way to his deputy Tun Abdul Razak. Under the Tunku's reign, UMNO was firm, but moderate, on the question of Malay privileges. It received the overwhelming majority of the Malay vote in every state and parliamentary election between 1955 and 1964, except the East Coast states where the more extremist Pan Malayan Islamic Party (or PMIP, currently known as Partai Islam) has often held sway. This support was undermined in the 1969 parliamentary election in which UMNO's vote declined to an estimated 41.4 percent of the total Malay vote, compared with 40.2 percent for the PMIP.[15] UMNO lost seven of the fifty-eight seats obtained in 1964, a substantial comedown. The losses can be attributed to the electoral appeal of the PMIP's campaign—a more vigorous defense and advocacy of Malay interests.

The PMIP is also exclusively Malay, but less moderate. Its leaders recommend a theological monarchy in place of the current constitutional democracy, openly advance Malay interests, and invite foreigners—including Chinese and Indian citizens of Malaya—to return to their homelands. At one time or another, the PMIP has been the governing party in the states of Kelantan and Trengganu, and its relations with the central government have been of political interest because of the central government's power to award financial grants in aid to the states.

The one remaining Malay party, though much less important, is the Party Ra'ayat, a radical left wing organization that advocates socialist policies. The Party Ra'ayat combined briefly with the non-Malay Labor Party to form the Socialist Front but fared badly within the marriage. It ultimately adopted a Malay communal outlook and in late 1965 with-drew from the Socialist Front to go it alone. Its importance has been negligible.

Non-Malay parties still outnumber Malay parties. Until re-cently, the most important of these has been the Malayan Chinese Association (MCA). Founded and backed by conser-vative Chinese businessmen, it has remained the party of the professional, middle class, English-speaking Chinese commu-nity. Throughout most of its history, it has been an integral member of the Alliance Party, a coalition of UMNO, MCA, and the Malayan Indian Congress (MIC). The MCA has never been a grass roots, mass-supported party like UMNO; its role in the Alliance has more often involved providing campaign funds and legitimating its policies on behalf of the Chinese community. In the 1969 general election it suffered a resounding defeat, losing twenty of thirty-three parliamentary contests. After the results became known, Tan Siew-sin, its leader, announced that the MCA no longer felt itself able to enter into a coalition government with UMNO. The failure of the Alliance government to form for the first time since inde-pendence may have contributed to the breakdown of law and order and the need for a proclamation of emergency. MCA members have rejoined the cabinet since the restoration of Par-liament in early 1971, but their position depends more on the preferences of the Malay elite than on the support of the Chinese electorate.

Contributing heavily to the defeat of the MCA was the growing success of the more extreme-minded Chinese (cum Indian) communal parties. The Democratic Action Party, the People's Progressive Party, and the Gerakan Ra'ayat Malaysia (Malaysian People's Movement) were the major beneficiaries of declining MCA fortunes. The DAP is the descendant of the older Singapore-based People's Action Party, and its central theme is of a "'Malaysian Malaysia" in which no one commu-nity would enjoy special privileges. The PPP, as usual, stressed multilingualism and pointed to the discrimination practiced

under Alliance rule. The GRM's relatively noncommunal plat-
form had some success in Northwest Malaya and even captured the Penang state government, but the GRM has since
fallen into bickering, resulting in the withdrawal and suspension of its major Indian and Malay supporters.[16] The major
element in the success of these parties in 1969 was their essentially anti-Malay position—a position they will no longer
be allowed to embrace publicly. How they will fare without
the issue of special privileges remains to be seen.

Three additional parties remain to be identified, two
Chinese and one Indian. The most important of these is the
Labor Party, originally a party of left wing English-speaking
Chinese. The party finally came under the control of
Chinese-speaking Chinese and adopted a program for social-
ism (annoyingly like the Communist program put forward by
the guerrillas during the 1948–60 emergency). Its position
today is unclear. It boycotted the 1969 general elections, and
its major personalities have joined the other non-Malay parties. For a while it was the major opposition party in Malaya,
and it has been victimized by government. The harassing and
jailing of its leaders and restrictions on meeting and cam-
paigning severely limited its effectiveness and contributed to
the decision of party leaders to boycott the 1969 election.

That leaves the United Democratic Party, which was essentially the party of one man, Dr. Lim Chong Eu, now the titu-
lar leader of the Gerakan Ra'ayat Malaysia and also the current chief minister of Penang. The one Indian party is the
Malayan Indian Congress, a member of the Alliance coalition. Although two of its members serve in the cabinet, it is a
numerically unimportant party. Indians do not comprise a
majority in any of the Malayan electoral districts. Moreover,
most Indians seem to prefer the non-Malay communal parties,
thereby siding with the Chinese on racial issues.

This brief account of the party system establishes that: *multiracial parties have invariably failed in competition with explicitly racial parties or coalitions of racial parties, and moder-*

ate parties over time have invariably fared worse in competition with the extremist racial parties.

KUALA LUMPUR AND PENANG

With the exception of brief side trips to Ipoh, Malacca, and the Borneo states of East Malaysia, I conducted almost all of my field research in Kuala Lumpur and Penang.[17] I lived in Kuala Lumpur from October 1966 through May 1967 and spent the following summer in Penang, returning briefly in December 1971 to gain some insight on the effects of the turmoil in Kuala Lumpur that followed the 13 May 1969 parliamentary elections. Although it is difficult to generalize about all of urban Malaya from the sample survey conducted in these two cities, the survey did obtain a substantial number of respondents, especially Chinese, in each of the cities and it thus permits a relatively sophisticated analysis of the responses. Few would disagree that Kuala Lumpur and Penang are Malaya's two most commerial and political cities. Kuala Lumpur is the site of the federal capital, and as Penang, after the 1969 election, was run by the Gerakan Ra'ayat Malaysia, it is interesting for our purposes.

The first and most obvious feature of both these cities is their Chinese character. Except for the Moorish architecture that dominates the railway station, the national bank, and the Selangor state government buildings in Kuala Lumpur, each of the cities could pass for a Chinese city located almost anywhere in Asia where the Chinese are heavily concentrated in urban areas. The Malay land reservations are not ostentatiously apparent, and they are anomalous in the overall physical appearance of these cities. The precise extent of Chinese domination is shown in Table 5.

There are a number of differences between the two cities. Large numbers of foreign diplomatic and business personnel reside in the federal capital, which accounts for the marginally higher percentage and absolutely greater number of "Others" under Kuala Lumpur. Substantially more Malays live in Kuala Lumpur, many of them engaged in government administration at various levels; the federal bureaucracy, with its Malay employees, operates from Kuala Lumpur. There are more Indians in Kuala Lumpur, mainly employed in transport (especially the railway) and communications—again, Kuala

Table 5 RACIAL COMPOSITION OF KUALA LUMPUR AND PENANG BY PERCENTAGES

Race	$(N=451,810)$ Kuala Lumpur	$(N=269,247)$ Penang
Malays	25.2	13.8
Chinese	54.8	71.6
Indians	18.6	13.3
Others	1.4	1.3

Sources: *1970 Population and Housing Census of Malaysia, Community Groups,* Table 9, p. 180; Table 12, p. 193; and Appendix I, p. 287.

Note: When the surrounding urban areas are included, the greater Kuala Lumpur population increases to 708,191 and the metropolitan Penang population to 331,763. However, the racial composition of the larger conurbations is virtually identical to that of the legal, gazetted cities (see Appendix 1).

Lumpur is the center for these industries. Commerce, manufacturing, trade, and mining are mainly the preserve of Chinese, and the greater proportion found in Penang suggests that the city is chiefly a business and trading community. Like Singapore, Penang was founded as a free port and developed chiefly as an entrepôt port and shopping center, though today many of these free port provisions have been eliminated (to the dismay of the Penang business community). Many of the Chinese in Penang seriously discussed independence for themselves (like Singapore) during the constitutional talks that created the Federation of Malaya. Although British officials were not receptive, Penang still retains a more British cum Chinese character than Kuala Lumpur.*

An interesting survey of squatters was carried out in Kuala Lumpur in 1964.[18] The survey estimated the total squatter population of the federal capital to be 105,000 persons, or more than one-fourth of the city's residents. As expected Chinese were the vast majority, comprising 69 percent. Malays made up 20 percent, and the remaining 11 percent were Indians. Note that the percentage of each race here roughly coincides with the overall racial composition of the city. It is difficult to tell from visual inspection of squatters' homes which race is more well-to-do. Although Malays maintain a cleaner, more attractive environment, the Chinese often prefer to invest their resources in jewelry and gold. It is not uncommon to see automobiles parked in front of the Chinese squatter's home.

Topographically, Kuala Lumpur is a city in which a small group of administrators and commercial officials of all races live in large houses in the hilly parts of the city or along Ampang Road, while the mass of residents live in racially segregated communities on the lowlands and in the center of town. Much of the commercial and administrative life of the city is crowded into a very small portion of Kuala Lumpur's thirty-six square miles; the density of population in one area of the business center exceeds 300,000 per square mile.[19]

Penang is residentially quite similar to Kuala Lumpur. The affluent of each race live in spacious homes and multiracial neighborhoods away from the congested center of town, while the vast majority of Penangites live in racially segregated communities in the crowded heart of town; population densities exceed 100,000 per square mile in the older sections.

The public opinion poll I commissioned tapped respondents

---

* In Kuala Lumpur, commercial advertisements for movies are in English, Malay, and Chinese; in Penang, only rarely in Malay. This is sensible from the point of view of market research; it also reveals something of the nature of the two cities.

in both the affluent multiracial neighborhoods as well as the more congested segregated areas. The effects of integrated versus segregated living upon racial attitudes and stereotypes is thus amenable to systematic evaluation.

— 3 —

An Overview of Malayan Politics

This chapter, an interpretation of the political process in postwar Malaya, provides a background for understanding how racial values, attitudes, stereotypes, and local urban politics fit the mosaic of political communalism in Malaya.* A general conception of politics is followed by a series of assumptions that capture the flavor of the multiracial situation. Next, five major features are listed that constitute the author's overview of Malayan politics, accompanied by illustrations from postwar and especially postindependence Malayan politics. A brief review of the literature on parties, elections, and contemporary Malayan politics is presented in Appendix 2. Data on the registration of social organizations is contained in Appendix 3.

---

* The overview in this chapter first appeared in Alvin Rabushka and Kenneth A. Shepsle, "Political Entrepreneurship and Patterns of Democratic Instability in Plural Societies," *Race* 12, no. 4 (April 1971):461–76. A formal exposition of the assumptions about plural societies and the five-stage paradigm of plural societies may be found in Alvin Rabushka and Kenneth A. Shepsle, *Politics in Plural Societies*, chaps. 2 and 3. This chapter attempts to summarize the highlights of the argument previously developed to set forth what I think the spirit of Malayan politics entails. It enables me to explain the significance of the changes that have taken place in local politics (see chapter 5) and to illuminate the relationship between racial values and political change in Malaya.

A CONCEPTION OF POLITICS

The ideal society, in the author's view, is one in which all choices are made in a market situation, on the basis of supply and demand. In this manner we buy food, shelter, clothing, cars, appliances, securities, and so forth. But for reasons of technology or cost, markets often fail to supply other things that we would like to purchase—among them national defense, law and order, and perhaps funding of professors' wages and research grants. The latter are known as publicly-supplied goods—i.e., they are paid for out of governmental revenues normally derived from taxation. What chiefly distinguishes publicly-supplied from market-supplied goods is that governments can use coercion to collect taxes, whereas in the free market individuals may choose to buy or not.

What this has to do with politics is that if all decisions were made on the basis of the voluntary exchange in free markets, there would be no politics as we understand the term. Fortunately or unfortunately, governments do more than provide defense, law and order, and underwrite professors' livelihoods. They also regulate air traffic control, automobile safety standards, the building and maintenance of roads, hospitals and schools, to name a few. We therefore need some way to convert individual preferences concerning these commodities into a social, or public, choice. Much like the marketplace, which converts the demand of consumers and the supply of producers into a market price for any given commodity, governments also make choices that represent an aggregate of individual preferences.

The author prefers to view politics in terms of choice. People often seek to have their own preferences concerning commodities, outcomes, and moral values imposed upon the whole of society, and this is normally accomplished through governments. Some public-choice decision rule, which may range from absolute dictatorship to complete unanimity, is required to translate individual preferences into a public choice. The scope of public choice may be either narrow or far-reaching, but it is independent of the decision-rule itself. For example, a dictator may force free markets and minimum government on all citizens, whether they like it or not. On the other hand, majority-rule democracies may vote to eliminate free markets and socialize the entire economy. The method of selecting those who exercise power can be quite independent of the use of that power. How the power figures are selected, and by whatever decision-rule public choices are made, public choices invariably result. The outcomes that result are the stuff of politics. In many societies, politics is of great importance in precisely those areas in which markets might suffice, e.g., housing, jobs, and education. In multiracial or plural societies, and especially in the less affluent ones, governmental control over the limited income opportunities that exist makes the fight for political power and the concern over political outcomes doubly vital.

Individual preferences, inferred from the choices people make in both public and private activities, thus underlies my conception of society. When these preferences result in a public choice, we have politics. The outcomes of public choices bear directly upon the legitimacy of government. If the outcomes are consistently favorable, the citizens of a society will accord their government legitimacy; if the reverse is true, they probably will not. Proclaiming the wonders of democratic or constitutional procedures on the basis of those who benefit from the outcomes of public choice will not long deceive those who consistently lose, or who subjectively see themselves as worse off. What all this means for the study of racial politics in Malaya is that our attention rightly belongs on the outcome of choices made by leaders of government with respect to national language policy, racial job quotas, racial scholarship quotas, etc., rather than on the procedures by which public choices are made. This is why we do not investigate how a bill becomes a law, but rather what the law states and how it subsequently affects individual preferences and behavior.

The author believes that human nature is motivated by self-interest and that individuals are the best judges of their own self-interest; they know their own preferences, however they arrive at them and are generally able to select alternatives by which their preferences will be realized. Individual choice is essentially rational, but rationality should not be confused with conventional moral judgments. It may be perfectly rational for an individual to initiate a race riot, for example, if his first preference is to do away with infidels. Preferences are taken as given, and their characteristics in the plural society are defined below.

PREFERENCES IN THE PLURAL SOCIETY

The individuals in a plural society also have preferences and a concern with political outcomes. When racial divisions become politically salient, it is important to understand these preferences.

Four assumptions characterize racial preferences in the plural society: intracommunal concensus, intercommunal conflict, perceptual concensus, and intense ethnic preferences. *Intracommunal consensus* means that all individuals of a given race perceive and express their preferences about political alternatives identically. For analytical purposes, then, a racial group is no different from any one of its members insofar as political preferences are concerned. Obviously, this does not preclude individual tastes in diet, music, clothing, or automobile color. It does, however, ascribe a uniformity of political preference to the members of the race.

Intercommunal conflict means that races disagree on all political issues facing the community. This gives a Hobbesian flavor to plural societies—a war of one race against the other

or of all races against each other. Again, this need not apply
in market exchange. It applies only when the public choices
that governments make are forced on all the citizens of a society, including those who oppose them. In Malaya's plural
society, this assumption is satisfied by the issues of language,
special privileges, and citizenship.

Perceptual consensus means that all races understand the
alternatives and how they favor one or another community.
Members of each race are well aware of the value incompati-
bilities between the races and know that a favorable outcome
for one race means an unfavorable outcome for another. In
short, in the plural society the lines of conflict are drawn, so-
lidified, and visible to everyone.

Finally, *intense ethnic preferences* means that members of
each race will sustain high risk to obtain their preferred cultural outcome. This assumption is crucial to an explanation of
both cooperative and competitive behavior between different
races.[1]

This characterization of preferences in the multiracial plural society, as it is revealed through political action, supports
the paradigm of racial politics in Malaya that follows.

FIVE FEATURES OF THE POLITICAL PROCESS
IN MALAYA'S PLURAL SOCIETY

Most plural societies, including Malaya, regularly exhibit
five features in their politics. These features are related to the
concept of racial preference just developed and are useful in
coming to grips with the workings of Malayan politics.

Preindependence racial cooperation. Most postindependence nationalist movements in plural societies were dominated
by elitist multiracial organizations. Led by the middle class,
which was in close contact with colonial officials—indeed,
many of the native middle class were educated in the mother

country—the multiracial independence movement displayed a convincing unity of purpose and an absence of interracial friction. The middle classes knew that interracial strife would only prolong colonial rule and delay independence; to hasten independence they cooperated with one another across racial lines.

The history of postwar Malaya is illustrative. British officials indicated that they would not grant independence to Malaya until the emergence of one or more responsible parties commanding broad support from all the races. Although the United Malays National Organization (UMNO) commanded widespread Malay support—having overturned the Malayan Union and thus preserved Malay political supremacy—it could not become the party of independence unless it could attract some non-Malay support. Accordingly, for convenience, it joined with the Malayan Chinese Association (MCA) to contest the Kuala Lumpur municipal elections in 1952 under the name of the Alliance Party, which won nine of twelve elective seats.

This coalition persisted through the spate of local elections subsequently held throughout the nation and received its ultimate test in 1955, when fifty-two elective Legislative Council seats were at stake. Since fifty seats had to be won to make up an elected majority (forty-six of the ninety-eight seats were non-elective), this election could make or break the Alliance as the party of independence. As it happened, the party won an overwhelming victory, securing fifty-one of the fifty-two contested seats. Shortly thereafter, on 31 August 1957, Malaya earned its independence.

A look at the political opposition indicates how thoroughly the theme of multiracial cooperation had permeated Malayan politics. The only serious opposition to the Alliance came from the Party Negara, the party of Dato Onn bin Ja'afar, who had been UMNO's founder and former president. He had left UMNO because of its unwillingness to become explicitly multiracial instead of explicitly racial. British officials, however, were satisfied that the Alliance coalition of racial parties enjoyed popular support and was able to govern. This arrangement, however, was neither as stable nor as long lasting as the 1955 election results seemed to suggest. Although the Alliance held up for nearly a decade, by then its seams had begun to show.

Postindependence racial cooperation. Multiracial cooperation was thus institutionalized in the organization of the Alliance Party, and Alliance leaders tried to maintain their political preeminence in independent Malaya. When the colonial power had departed, however, Malayan politics became redistributive. Gains at the expense of one race became the rewards of racial politics for the victors. In retrospect, it seems only reasonable that politicians would champion the cause of their own respective races.

But the multiracial nationalists—in this case the members of the Alliance Party—fought to retain their governing position by employing two techniques to protect themselves from communal strain inherent even within the organization itself. On the one hand, they stressed such national issues as economic development and territorial integrity; on the other hand, they treated communal issues ambiguously.

By stressing national issues, the Alliance Party could avoid divisive politics. Parties appealing to the racial interests of the separate communities were accused of undercutting national development and unity and even, on occasion, of treason. In 1959 the Alliance, calling itself the party of independence, campaigned on the theme of steady economic growth. In 1964 its leaders stressed confrontation with Indonesia, characterizing opposing racial parties as traitors who sought to aid and comfort the nation's enemies. When this tactic was used again in 1969, however it fell on deaf ears.

The second technique entailed treating divisive racial issues ambiguously. As suggested earlier, individuals in the plural society have intense racial preferences, so that it is possible for groups with incompatible preferences to entertain a common ambiguous appeal.* Gordon P. Means shows how the Alliance employed ambiguity in its 1959 electoral campaign.

> During that campaign the Alliance leadership exhibited some ambivalence toward communal issues. On the one hand Tunku Abdul Rahman made a communal appeal for the support of the Malays, stressing such issues as "the alien danger" and the threat to the Malays posed by the immigration of "foreigners." On the other hand, he defended the Alliance manifesto which attributed the "alien danger" to the restrictive citizenship requirements which made it difficult for non-Malays to acquire full status as Malayan citizens. Thus, the Alliance tended to utilize the "foreign threat" issue in appealing to the Malays, but hastened to explain to its [Malayan Chinese Association and Malayan Indian Congress] members that the loyal Chinese and Indians in these two organizations were not a part of that "foreign threat." *This is just one of the many examples of ambiguous terms being employed successfully to keep incongruous elements united for common political action* [italics mine].[2]

The growing salience of race and the rise of the political entrepreneur. Ultimate loyalty in the plural society is *racial,* not *national.* Though appeals to national issues produce immediate results, they often fail in the long run. Only the ability to cope with the racial issue enables the multiracial coalition to survive.

For these reasons, ambitious politicians sense the appeal of the racial issue and sooner or later succeed in making it the sole salient issue in politics. Why race instead of some less inflammatory theme, such as waste or inefficiency in government? The answer depends on historical circumstance. Sometimes the politician is captive to an extremist outlook in his electorate. On other occasions he may be inciting extremism, e.g., the Reverend Ian Paisley in Northern Ireland. It is not clear

---

* The formal proof is contained in Rabushka and Shepsle, *Politics in Plural Societies,* chap. 3 and is not reproduced here.

which of these possibilities best fits Malaya, but there is no doubt that the race issue increased in importance and culminated in the Alliance's first serious losses in 1969, when an attempt to focus on national issues failed to neutralize the volatile appeal of race.

Outbidding and the decline of the multiracial coalition. When national issues are paramount, the position of the multiracial coalition as the only national party is secure. Its position becomes more tenuous, however, as the prominence of racial issues increases. A victorious strategy for the communal politician involves only two steps: (1) increasing the salience of racial issues, and then (2) outbidding the ambiguous multiracial coalition on those issues.

Let us explore the implications of this approach for the politics of moderation. As long as national issues predominate, the multiracial coalition can play down, or even avoid, racial questions. Disregard of *salient* racial issues, however, may be politically fatal. In 1969, for example, UMNO confronted an appeal from the Pan Malayan Islamic Party (PMIP) that emphasized Alliance failures in promoting Malay interests. Many Malays evidently believed that twelve years of Alliance rule had not brought them substantial gains, and an appeal for national unity could no longer neutralize these racial sentiments. For UMNO to counter effectively the racial appeal of the PMIP required that it, too, adopt a racial outlook. To have done so, however, would have severely strained the weak ties holding the multiracial Alliance together. The same argument applies to the Malayan Chinese Association (MCA). To combat extremist Chinese parties on their own terrain would make the MCA's relationship with UMNO even more precarious. Moreover, the Alliance's credibility was established only on national issues. Why should the electorate buy a racial appeal from the hitherto moderate multiracial party? Politicians in the Alliance were damned if they did and damned if they didn't.*

* A crisis had erupted in July 1959 over the allocation of seats within the Alliance Party. An MCA demand for forty seats was con-

UMNO lost eight seats, mainly to the PMIP, and watched the PMIP percentage of the total Malay vote climb to nearly its own. Even more dramatically, the MCA lost twenty of thirty-three contests to the extremist Chinese parties. After the election, MCA president Tun Tan Siew-sin announced that he and members of his party could no longer sit in concert with UMNO in the new cabinet. Democracy immediately became untenable. Law and order broke down in Kuala Lumpur, and martial law was declared.[3] Parliament was dissolved, though it was later restored in February 1971. Thus, a politics of racial outbidding seemed logically to imply the demise of the moderate multiracial coalition. To fight extremists on their own grounds threatens the internal bonds within the multiracial party; to refuse the challenge results in electoral defeat. In retrospect, the Alliance leadership may be credited with having maintained itself successfully from 1952 until 1969.

Electoral manipulations and the politics of redistribution. Once in power, political leaders are not averse to rewriting the rules of democratic politics to suit their own interests. A variety of manipulative practices is available: outlawing opposing parties, restricting social organizations,* jailing political opponents, suspending elections and constitutionally elected bodies (permissible under Malaya's emergency regulations), or amending the constitution. The latter is perfectly legal, however unfair to one or more of the races. It has already been seen that a Malay-majority parliament amended the constitution to increase the potential representation of heavily-Malay rural constituencies. It will be seen later that Parliament, together with Alliance-ruled state governments, dissolved locally

sidered too large by UMNO, and the Alliance was in momentary danger of dissolution. After the Tunku's stern personal intervention, the crisis was resolved but not until MCA president Dr. Lim Chong Eu was forced to resign along with many of his more militant supporters. For details, see Gordon P. Means, *Malaysian Politics* (New York: New York University Press, 1970), pp. 212–15.

* Appendix 3 contains information about lawfully registered societies, by race, from 1959 through 1971.

elected councils, which were administered for the most part by
opposition Chinese parties. More recent, and far more pro-
found, are the Constitutional Amendment Act of 1971 and
the 1969 revision of the Sedition Act; together they provide
that anyone who publicly questions Malay special privileges
can be convicted of sedition and appropriately punished. The
raison d'être of the opposition communal parties (the PMIP,
PPP, DAP, GRM, etc.) had been the interests of the respective races. Now these parties are forbidden by law to raise issues of race in subsequent campaigns. In short, the most salient political issue in Malaya is now constitutionally
proscribed.*

Constitutional and other manipulative procedures are one
method for ensuring the retention of power (especially if the
police and the army are racially akin to the elected or appointed rulers). One reason for working so hard to keep
power lies in the control of public finance, namely, the collection of taxes and the expenditure of revenues. As has already
been mentioned, governments are unique in being able to
coerce their citizens into buying publicly-supplied goods,
whether they want them or not.

More specifically, public revenues pay for national mu-
seums, national mosques, highways, railroads, irrigation projects, rural land development schemes, electrification projects,
rural health programs, state development corporations, urban

---

* Without this measure, the Alliance Party would probably have
suffered additional losses in subsequent elections, assuming that race
remained politically salient. By prohibiting a politics of race, they may
have restored national issues to a position of salience and at the same
time dramatically improved their future prospects. My own hunch is
that a large number of non-Malay voters will either abstain in future
elections, having correctly recognized that the important issues in Malaya are no longer open to democratic resolution via the ballot box, or
perhaps join Chin Peng in the jungle. Given the current ban on the issues of race, what democracy now entails in Malaya is quite different
from the original 1957 *merdeka* constitution. When the major issues
of a society are legally proscribed, they may erupt through extralegal
channels, e.g., terrorism and rebellion.

development authorities, national corporations (e.g., Pernas), and even mosquito abatement, among other things, and these projects chiefly benefit Malays. A reading of the annual and development expenditures of government reveals numerous schemes designed chiefly to aid rural Malays; we have already seen how the constitution aids urban Malays in civil service appointments, university scholarships, and business permits and licenses. While it is difficult to establish exactly how many public dollars are spent to benefit Malays, it can be shown how few dollars Malays pay into the public coffers.*

A good deal is known, on the other hand, about the collection of taxes. Much valuable information can be found in an excellent study by C. T. Edwards entitled *Public Finances in Malaya and Singapore,* which focuses almost entirely on taxation.[4] Edwards shows, for example, that Malays paid only 6.4 percent of all personal income tax collected in 1964, compared with 51.6 percent for Chinese, 11.0 percent for Indians and 31.0 percent for non-Asians and non-residents.[5] Since personal tax rates rise progressively with income, non-Asians are subject to higher marginal and average rates of tax than

* This is especially difficult to compute for recurrent budget expenditure. Estimates of racial allocations in development expenditures are somewhat easier to compute, but these are at best, very rough. I have tried estimating the racial intents behind the budget categories for the *First* and *Second Malaysia Plans.* Using "rule of thumb" procedures for estimation, I was surprised to discover that the percentages in the two plans designated chiefly to benefit Malays were nearly identical (though the greater absolute size of the second plan means that more real dollars are allocated for Malays). My "guesstimate" comes to about 65 percent for both plans, which means that Malays, who make up just over half the population, will receive more than their pro rata share of the population would warrant. Why then all the publicity given the New Economic Policy, the stated position of government to uplift the position of the Malays? Evidently to pacify Malay opinion. An analysis of the breakdown of the two development plans reveals that the *Second Malaysia Plan* provides for more visibly concentrated pro-Malay expenditures: Pernas, Urban Development Authority, State Development Corporations. Malay development expenditures during the first plan tended to be more evenly (hence invisibly) distributed throughout the countryside.

Asians, and, within the Asian community, Chinese pay at a higher rate than Malays.[6] In the area of corporate taxation, he reports that almost half of the total company tax is paid by non-Asian firms, the balance being paid principally by the Chinese.[7] Export taxes, making up about M$182 million (out of a total government tax revenue of M$1,377 million in 1968), are levied chiefly on rubber and tin, whose ownership is mainly non-Malay. Import duties, comprising M$563 million, are also paid chiefly by non-Malays. The same is true of excise taxes, indirect taxes, and a 5 percent development tax levied on business firms. Though exact figures have not been computed, it would be surprising if the total Malay contribution to federal, state, and local taxes was anywhere near 10 percent. Undoubtedly more than 10 percent of public spending is geared to help Malays, and it is, therefore, easy to see why Malays are concerned about their political position and the power of redistribution it commands.

Although Edwards avoids moral judgments, he is not blind to the potential for redistribution of wealth by government.

> The communal division of the population largely explains the high degree of centralization of government power in Malaya. The Malays, although politically dominant in each of the eleven States, realize that it is easier to retain indefinite control over one central government than over eleven separate State governments. In addition, they recognize that, with central control over a wide range of policies, the redistribution of income from the richer to the poorer, more backward, and predominantly Malay States is possible.[8]

Earlier in the book, Edwards notes that the public sector in Malaya had become responsible for 24 percent of gross national expenditure by 1965, which was more than double the share of total expenditure undertaken by the government in 1950. For Edwards, the postwar period witnessed a significant increase in the influence of the government—a Malay government—over the level and composition of domestic activity.[9] The steady growth of the public sector lends indirect but confirming evidence that Malay control over the economy, and control over Chinese business activity as well, is steadily increasing.

However, a compelling argument can be made—indeed often has been made—that stability and harmony cannot come to Malaya until the races achieve a more equitable economic and political balance. Free market forces are unlikely to bring this economic balance into being. Some scholars therefore cling to the belief that a substantial amount of government assistance is needed to redress the economic imbalance between the races, and this entails having the Chinese and non-Asians pay both the economic and political costs involved.

Interracial Values and
Social Behavior

Here we begin to understand the Malayan man in the street
—his social behavior, racial values and beliefs, and later his
political behavior and preferences—by means of this first
(although exclusively urban) systematic assessment of mass
values and opinions undertaken in Malaya. Indians are ex-
cluded from most of the analysis for two reasons: first, because the number of Indian respondents is less than would be
desired for rigorous statistical analysis; secondly, because
Indians are a marginal community in Malaya and are unimportant in the mainstream of Malayan politics. For analytical
purposes, it is a useful simplification to view the urban community as Chinese and Malay.

THE RESPONDENTS

Racially, the respondents reasonably reflect the overall
demographic configuration in the two cities. As seen in Table
6, the Chinese are overrepresented in Kuala Lumpur and
underrepresented in Penang. For Malays, the situation is re-
versed. Regarding religion, all Malyas in both cities are Muslims (as required by Malaya's constitution), two-thirds of the

Table 6   RACIAL COMPOSITION OF RESPONDENTS
IN KUALA LUMPUR AND PENANG
COMPARED WITH CENSUS DISTRIBUTIONS,
BY PERCENTAGES

Kuala Lumpur		
	(N = 359)	(N = 452,000)
Race	Sample	Census (1970)
Malays	13.3	25.2
Chinese	74.9	54.8
Indians	8.9	18.6

Penang		
	(N = 374)	(N = 269,000)
Race	Sample	Census (1970)
Malays	16.8	13.8
Chinese	67.4	71.6
Indians	13.9	13.3

Note: Although I do not have exact figures, the Kuala Lumpur population has recently shown a dramatic increase in the number of
Malays. At the time of the survey (1967), Malays were estimated to comprise no more than 20 percent of Kuala Lumpur's
population (in 1957, they made up only 15 percent). The
Chinese percentage should be adjusted upward correspondingly
to obtain the correct 1967 figure.

Chinese practice Buddhism or Taoism, and more than half the
Indians in each city are Hindus.

The sexual composition of the sample is nearly identical in
each city. For Malays, the number of male and female respondents was about equal. For Chinese, the ratio of female to
male was about sixty-forty, which suggests that many Chinese
housewives were interviewed during the day when their hus-
bands were away at work. As to education, few respondents in
either city had completed a university degree; about one-third
of the respondents in both cities had no schooling at all; and
no one racial group produced the greater proportion of highly
educated persons. (The quality of education cannot be judged,
since information was not collected on the type of school at-

tended, e.g., English, or Chinese, Malay, and Tamil vernacular schools.)

RACIAL BEHAVIOR

Although direct observation on some systematic basis would produce the most valid information concerning the nature of interracial contact between Chinese and Malays, I attempted to obtain this information during the interview. Respondents were asked to report their usual social behavior. Table 7 was compiled from responses to the question:

> Outside of your immediate family, what types of people do you normally mix with (IF "Everyone" or "Everybody" PROBE FOR COMBINATIONS)
> > Malays
> > Chinese
> > Indians
> > Eurasians
> > Others (write in combinations)

The respondent is asked only to recall his *current* daily patterns of behavior, and one assumes that he is capable of giving an accurate description.

Two striking patterns emerge. First, the citizens of Kuala Lumpur are more outgoing than their counterparts in Penang, which gives credence to the view that Kuala Lumpur is a more cosmopolitan community than Penang; it houses the bulk of the foreign diplomatic and business community and is more socially permissive—indeed, Penang seems almost quaint and stodgy by comparison. Secondly, and more significantly for our purposes, in both cities the vast majority of Chinese seem to prefer to keep to themselves in their daily social activities, while Malays, on the other hand, are much more outgoing.

These results are understandable to anyone who has lived

Table 7   SOCIAL BEHAVIOR PATTERNS IN
KUALA LUMPUR AND
PENANG BY PERCENTAGES

Kuala Lumpur		
	(N = 48)	(N = 269)
Behavior Pattern	*Malays*	*Chinese*
Social Introverts	22.9	68.8
Social Extroverts	75.0	29.4
Penang		
	(N = 63)	(N = 252)
Behavior Pattern	*Malays*	*Chinese*
Social Introverts	31.7	79.0
Social Extroverts	68.3	20.6

Note: Some ambiguous responses defeated easy classification into introvert or extrovert. Hence, percentages do not always total 100.

for any length of time in either city. The Chinese can spend an entire day shopping, learning, visiting, or eating with their own people. Malays are less restricted socially because the cities are chiefly Chinese in composition. Few Malays can eat, shop, and conduct their daily affairs exclusively in the company of other Malays. They are forced, as it were, into a more extensive interracial mixing than the Chinese. How this affects urban racial values and beliefs will be seen shortly.

CULTURAL ETHNOCENTRISM

By "cultural ethnocentrism" is meant how keenly the Chinese and Malays feel about the importance of their own culture. This information was obtained in response to the question:

Some people say that one way of life is superior to another. Others say there is little difference. In your opinion which way of life do you consider the best?

Malay way of life
Chinese way of life
Indian way of life
Western or European way of life
Others (write in)

Table 8 shows that Chinese are more ethnocentric than Malays, though the pattern is far more pronounced in Penang. Malays in Kuala Lumpur may be more aware of their own culture because of the presence of the *Dewan Bahasa dan Pustaka* (National Language and Literature Agency) and other centers of Malay cultural activity, e.g., the National Mosque, the National Museum, and the National University. In any case, given the much older and more established character of Chinese culture, these results accord with expectations.

Table 8   CULTURAL ETHNOCENTRISM AMONG MALAYS
AND CHINESE BY PERCENTAGES

Kuala Lumpur	
(N = 47)	*(N = 264)*
Malays	*Chinese*
64	68
Penang	
(N = 63)	*(N = 251)*
Malays	*Chinese*
48	90

When the data in Table 8 are analyzed on the basis of the respondent's social behavior—i.e., did he stay among his own kind or cross racial boundaries in his daily living patterns—it is found that social introverts of both races are more enthusiastic about their own culture than social extroverts.* In other words, interracial social interaction reduces cultural ethnocentrism.

* To avoid cluttering the text with tables, results based on second- and third-order controls are verbally summarized.

SOCIAL DISTANCE: TOLERATION

Analysts of Malaya usually assume that mutual fear and distrust characterize interracial activities. To put it another way, it might be asked how tolerant the two communities are of each other. A standard technique is to use some form of the Bogardus "social distance" scale, which is designed to measure how willing the members of one community are to relate to another. A modified scale was constructed for this Malayan interview.

> I am going to describe some situations to you and I want to know your own reactions.
> Would you like it or not if you were eating at the same restaurant as (READ OUT IN TURN)
> > an average Chinese
> > an average Malay
> > an average Indian
> . . . . if you had to work with?
> . . . . if you belonged to the same organization with?
> . . . . if your neighbor was?
> . . . . if someone from your own family married?

Table 9 shows the results for Malay respondents in both cities. Because of the Islamic proscription of pork for Malays, and because Chinese prefer pork to most other meats, few Malays report that they are willing to eat with Chinese. Here the religious barrier is reflected in "social distance" from a Malay point of view. Employment and social activity percentages are considerably higher, reinforcing the conclusion that religion does affect the issue of restaurants. Penang Malays are more tolerant of the Chinese than their Kuala Lumpur counterparts, but they are less tolerant on the question of interracial marriage. But omitting eating and marriage, the two associations affected by religion, we find (with one exception) that two-thirds of all Malay respondents are not opposed to crossing racial boundaries in employment, social activity, or neighborhood of residence.

Table 9   MALAY TOLERATION (SOCIAL DISTANCE) TOWARDS CHINESE BY PERCENTAGES

Relationships	(N = 47) Kuala Lumpur	(N = 63) Penang
Eating at the same restaurant	47	44
Working at the same job	72	79
Belonging to same organization	70	68
Neighborhood proximity	53	67
Marriage	49	32

Note: The table is read as follows: of the Malays in Kuala Lumpur, 47 percent are willing to eat with Chinese, 72 percent are willing to work at the same job with Chinese, and so forth.

The Chinese-Malay results are more interesting. Excluding marriage, the Chinese responses appear in Table 10.* When compared with Table 9, one notes two outstanding differences. First, no religious obstacle impedes the Chinese from eating with Malays in the same eating house. Though Malay aversion to pork may restrict their choice of eating house, the Chinese are extremely willing to eat with Malays. Secondly, the Chinese percentages (with one exception) are consistently higher than those obtained for Malays. Stated differently, Chinese in both Kuala Lumpur and Penang are more tolerant of Malays than Malays are tolerant of them. In greater degree, they are willing to eat, work, join, and live with members of the Malay race.**

    * Chinese respondents were unhappy about this question. Since the law requires all non-Malays who marry Malays to be Muslim converts, most Chinese (about 75 percent in each city) would not like their children to intermarry with Malays. As mentioned in chapter 2, intermarriage has been slight in Malayan history; see Alvin Rabushka, "Intermarriage in Malaya," pp. 103–108.
    ** When these data were broken down by patterns of racial interaction, it was found that Chinese social extroverts (those who

Table 10 CHINESE TOLERATION (SOCIAL DISTANCE)
TOWARDS MALAYS BY PERCENTAGES

Relationships	(N = 264) Kuala Lumpur	(N = 251) Penang
Eating at the same restaurant	77	73
Working at the same job	77	75
Belonging to same organization	73	71
Neighborhood proximity	77	77

The Chinese, then, are more ethnocentric than Malays and at the same time more tolerant of them than are Malays of Chinese. The explanation of this duality may lie in the Chinese historical experience. Descendants of the dominant Asian civilization, they are more self-confident, more cosmopolitan, and more accustomed to dealing with outsiders. In any event, distrust and hostility seems to be more characteristic of Malays than of Chinese. (Appendix 4 presents another interpretation of these data.)

STEREOTYPES

Much has been made of racial stereotypes and how the holding of inaccurate and degrading views is detrimental to social harmony.* The author believes, however, that, at least in the Malayan context, racial stereotypes play little or no role in influencing social or political harmony.** More interesting is

cross racial lines) were by far more tolerant of Malays than Chinese introverts. The same was true of Malay introverts and extroverts. Again, social mingling seemed positively correlated with social distance.

* This material first appeared as "Racial Sterotypes in Malaya," *Asian Survey* 11, no. 7 (July 1971):709–16.

** It is shown elsewhere that Chinese and Malays like or dislike each other independently of stereotypes. A "good" image neither improves the relations between the races nor improves the actual rate of mingling across racial lines; see Alvin Rabushka, "Affective, Cognitive the question of to what extent the stereotypes held by the population conform to the views held by outside analysts of Malayan society. For this reason an attempt was made during the survey to obtain information about racial stereotypes. What do members of each racial group think about themselves and about members of the other races?

The interview items were designed after a careful reading of the existing literature on Malayan stereotypes. T. H. Silcock, for example, advances the view that "The Chinese firmly believe that their wealth and Malay poverty are the natural consequences of Chinese industry, thrift, and adaptability to modern ways, and of Malay indolence, thriftlessness, and conservatism." [1] This is similar to the view offered by Gayl Ness.

> It is widely believed that the Chinese are achievement-oriented, industrious, opportunistic, avaricious, and are sharp business men. Malays are held to lack achievement orientation, to be lazy, and to show a distaste of hard labor. At the same time they are believed to be loyal, polite and proud. The Chinese are held to be self-possessed, the Malays headstrong and erratic. The Chinese are believed to be self-reliant, while the Malays rely upon government assistance and protection—a result of the spoon-feeding of colonial protection. The estate Indians are generally considered to be low in mental ability, lacking in self-reliance and achievement orientation. The urban commercial class of Indians, on the other hand, share many of the characteristics of the Chinese, especially in commercial and financial matters; they are not, however, thought to be as industrious or as work-oriented as the Chinese. [2]

These stereotypes are not new. Sir Frank Swettenham, a former colonial administrator, suggests of the Malay that

and Behavioral Consistency of Chinese-Malay Interracial Attitudes," *Journal of Social Psychology* 82 (October 1970):35–41.

he is . . . lazy to a degree, is without method or order of any kind, knows no regularity even in the hours of his meals, and considers time as of no importance. His house is untidy, even dirty, but he bathes twice a day, and is very fond of personal adornment in the shape of smart clothes.[3]

Peter Wilson sets forth the Malay villager's view of Chinese and Indians.

Malay villagers appear to hold to the opinion that all Chinese are dirty. The principal meaning implied is not so much physical dirtiness as ritual impurity, and this attitude finds its most powerful, symbolic expression in the contrast between the Malay injunction against the eating of pork because it is unclean and the extreme penchant of the Chinese for pork. . . . Thus, no matter how clean a Chinese may be, he is always ritually impure to the Malay.

In general, villagers seem to regard Indians as people to laugh about: the blackness of skin, hairiness, and the skinny men and fat women seemed to amuse them most. . . . Village men and women alike object to, or find most peculiar, the smells associated with Indians. Most Indian stores have an incense stick burning, and there is often blended in with this the smell of scent. The smell of Indian cooking seems characteristic to Malay villagers, to whom the body smell of Indians is also oppressive. A major reason given by villagers for not travelling on a bus at night is that the smell of Indians is so strong. . . . But whereas the Chinese are ritually or mystically dirty, Indians are considered squalid.[4]

Other reporters of stereotypes such as Tjoa Soei Hock[5] and Victor Purcell[6] offer comparable descriptions. At this point, it is useful to return to the survey to see how these views accord with those held by the mass of urban Malays and Chinese.

The pertinent question on the interview was phrased as follows:

I am going to mention some human qualities one at a time. Tell me frankly (PAUSE) what you think. First, take *AMBI-*

TION. Do you think that among the Chinese their amount of *ambition* is very high, high, low or very low? How about the Malays? How about the Indians?
Now take *ACTIVITY IN PUBLIC AND SOCIAL AFFAIRS.*
Now take *THRIFT.*
Now take *INTELLIGENCE.*
Now take *HONESTY.*
Now take *CLEANLINESS.*

To gain some measure of group stereotypes, numbers were assigned as follows: four points for a response of very high, three points for high, two for low, and one for very low. By adding and averaging point totals, a rank ordering of racial attributes could be produced. In almost every case, two of the three races held similar views about the personality attributes of the third. In other words, Malays and Indians see Chinese in the same light; Malay and Chinese views on Indians correspond closely; and Chinese and Indians describe Malays in the same terms. A genuine consensus on stereotypes holds across urban Malaya.

The Malays regard the Chinese as very intelligent, very ambitious, and quite active, with honesty, thrift, and cleanliness following in order of importance. The last entry, cleanliness, corroborates Wilson's description of Chinese ritual impurity as attested to by Malays. But the first two items, intelligence and ambition, are the features most often cited in the literature. We now have systematic evidence that these views are widespread among non-Chinese. Moreover, this ranking is very similar to the Chinese self-portrait.

How do Chinese see Malays? They are scored highest on cleanliness, and they are considered to lack ambition (the other characteristics follow no particular ordering). Intelligence, thrift, activity, and honesty are given approximately equal point values (by my scoring procedure) and fall significantly below the scores registered for cleanliness and (lack of) ambition.

If eradicating unfavorable stereotypes was beneficial to harmony and social stability, we might be concerned that the Chinese apparently regard Malays as indolent—i.e., would the Chinese take seriously a Malay government plan to bring Malays into the modern commercial sector of the economy? The adage holds that unfavorable stereotypes will be relinquished only when individuals know each other on a personal basis.

But information is costly, and stereotypes are economical devices for storing large amounts of information. Moreover, when the survey respondents are separated into social introverts and extroverts, no significant difference in stereotype scores results. Those who know more about members of the other race in Malaya do not hold a different view from those who confine themselves socially to their own kind. Finally, I could find no systematic connection between stereotype scores and an expressed willingness to associate with members of other races in restaurants, employment, social clubs, and residential neighborhoods. Efforts to eradicate stereotypes are simply not to the point; as far as I can tell, the holding of narrow stereotyped views in Malaya has no visible impact on either social interchange or political unity.

POLITICAL PROBLEMS

To complete this profile of the urban Malay and Chinese, the responses to one last question should be examined: "In your opinion what are the most important political problems facing Malaysia today? (PROBE: What else? AT LEAST ONE AND UP TO THREE)." This question was deliberately open-ended. We wanted to know what kinds of problems the respondent would identify as political, how many he would cite, and what proportion of these would have direct racial overtones.*

* It was anticipated that Malays would list Chinese economic power as an important issue from their perspective and that Chinese would

The results are revealing. First and most important, most of the respondents were unwilling to answer the question, and, as may clearly be seen in Table 11, surprisingly few could list more than one "political" issue. As mentioned in chapter 1, interviewers encountered resistance to this question. Malays

Table 11   NONRESPONSE BY MALAYS AND CHINESE
           (ON THE QUESTION OF POLITICAL ISSUES)
           BY PERCENTAGES

Kuala Lumpur		
	(N=47)	(N=264)
Number of Issues	Malays	Chinese
First Issue	32	48
Second Issue	47	72
Third Issue	72	92
Penang		
	(N=63)	(N=251)
Number of Issues	Malays	Chinese
First Issue	59	63
Second Issue	78	88
Third Issue	95	98

Note: This table should be read as follows: in Kuala Lumpur, 32 percent of the Malays would not list even one issue, 47 percent could not list two issues, 72 percent could not list three issues, and so forth.

were more willing than Chinese to volunteer answers, and both races in Kuala Lumpur were more willing than their Penang counterparts. Malays probably feel more politically secure than Chinese and were less fearful of responding to the question. And since politics plays a much larger role in Kuala

list the national language issue and other Malay rights from their point of view. These patterns had appeared in responses to a mailed questionnaire conducted at the University of Malaya from November 1966 to February 1967. University students in Malaya, however, are politically aware and often gave the responses they believed the question aimed to elicit.

Lumpur than in Penang, it is reasonable that Kuala Lumpur residents would have given more attention to political topics and be better able to respond to the question.

What, though, was the substantive content of the responses? Did they indicate concern with communal issues? second-class citizenship for Chinese? fear of Chinese economic power for Malays? In spite of the efforts of extremist political parties to sensitize the electorate on racial issues, most respondents expressed their "political" problems in "bread and butter" terms. Between 50 and 80 percent of all responses stressed low wages (for members of both races) and the problem of obtaining a good education for their children. Insofar as those responses that seemed concerned with communal issues could be identified at all, the percentages were generally below 10 for each race in both cities. To repeat, only a small fraction of the respondents commented on language, special privileges, citizenship, religion, quotas, etc., and no differences could be found between social introverts and extroverts. These responses suggest why the extremist parties did so well in the 1969 parliamentary election: they could accuse the Alliance of not making sufficient economic progress since independence because the MCA, the Chinese party, was the party of the rich business community and not of the ordinary Chinese citizen. By the same token, UMNO is the party of the Malay establishment and not the true expression of the Malay *ra'ayat*.

SUMMARY

One can now compose a portrait of the ordinary urban Chinese and Malay. The urban Chinese keeps to himself, is culturally very confident (ethnocentric), extremely tolerant of the Malay, views the Malay almost paternalistically, and, when willing to express himself, identifies the most important political problems in terms of daily economics. The urban Malay, on the other hand, is more outgoing, less culturally self-centered, and also less tolerant towards the Chinese. His political problems are no different from those of his Chinese countrymen: bad housing, costly schooling, high prices, unemployment, etc. Specifically political behavior and party preference are considered in the next chapter, in which political participation is related to racial values.

Several implications emerge from these racial profiles. First, the urban Chinese would probably be happier if left to himself. Secondly, the urban Malay is probably easiest to arouse on the communal issue because his tolerance threshold is lower than that of the Chinese.[7] (This seems consistent with John Slimming's account of the 1969 Kuala Lumpur race riots.) Thirdly, the genuine mass concern in *urban Malaya* is economic, even though it invariably takes on communal overtones. Warning the people about communal dangers, as Malayan government ministers so often do, is not likely to help put Humpty-Dumpty back together again.

— 5 —

Racial Politics in Microcosm

Chapter 5 examines the political behavior and beliefs of the urban Malay and Chinese on the basis of, first, a history of municipal politics in Kuala Lumpur and Penang; secondly, a review of parliamentary and state legislative assembly election results for the constituencies that comprise the two cities; and finally, an examination of the reported political behavior and party preferences of the survey respondents.

It should be noted in advance that the Malayan government did not consult the needs of modern social scientists in delineating its constituencies. Census and constituency boundaries do not coincide, and it is therefore difficult to correlate the population's social and economic characteristics with election results on a constituency-by-constituency basis. To attempt, moreover, to infer how individuals vote from an analysis of overall voting results will in all likelihood result in an "ecological fallacy." Suppose, for example, that 40 percent of the registered voters in any given constituency are Chinese and that Chinese candidates in that constituency receive 40 percent of the votes cast. To infer on that basis that all Chinese voted for candidates of their race does not follow. Any Chinese who voted for a Malay or Indian can have his vote offset in the aggregate by a Malay or Indian who crossed racial lines to vote for a Chinese. Inferences drawn about individual voting behavior from an analysis of aggregate results are thus suspect.

71

This does not mean that no conclusions are possible. On the contrary, general trends are discernible, but it is necessary to exercise caution with regard to individual imputations. Only a series of carefully completed surveys after each election would reveal changes in how individuals voted; in that regard, the author's survey gives some insight into the 1964 general elections. But on the basis of the discussion in chapter 3, the survey responses, and the aggregate data analyzed herein, the trends uncovered may confidently be regarded as correct.

LOCAL POLITICS

When British colonial authorities introduced local elections in Malaya in 1951 (beginning in Penang), they had in mind a kind of graduated citizenship or civics training exercise for its residents.[1] This is clearly stated on page 1 of the *Report on the Introduction of Elections in the Municipality of George Town, Penang, 1951.*

> The introduction of the modern type of democratic election, based on adult suffrage, has been made . . . carefully. It starts with local government and will, in due course, work outward and upward to Settlement, State, and Federal Councils. The transition from bureaucratic Local Government to a popularly elected Municipal Council has among its by-products the popularizing of the idea of registration, the training of registration and polling staff, and the holding of the first democratic elections in the Federation of Malaya.[2]

Explicit considerations of race are absent from this document, notwithstanding that Chinese comprise a majority of the urban populations. This is probably because of the need to obtain Chinese support for the colonial regime against the Communist territorists. It was believed that this support might be obtained by involving the Chinese in their own local affairs.

Before taking up specific elections in the two cities, it is necessary to set forth the constitutional foundations of local elections. Authorizing the first election was the *Local Authorities Election Ordinance of 1950*,[3] which provided that the ruler in council of a state or the high commissioner of a settlement (Penang or Malacca) could grant each municipality a constitution for a degree of home rule. The ordinance allowed state authorities to amend these municipal constitutions, but it *did not explicitly specify the power of revocation*. The same ordinance also provided for the establishment of town boards and rural boards for areas with smaller populations, but in these cases state authorities retained the right to revoke the boards and replace their elected members with appointees.

To extend greater democratic responsibility to the resettled Chinese, who had been moved from the fringes of the jungle in order that they could be more closely supervised and protected, additional machinery was put into effect. *The Local Councils Ordinance, 1952* provided for elected members to local councils, which differ from the town boards and rural boards authorized by the 1950 ordinance. In this case, state authorities retained the power of dissolution.

The idea behind the introduction of popular elections in Malaya was to expand the democratic process by a gradual introduction of local elections, moving next to state and federal elections if the former were successful. But in the process the British imparted a good deal of autonomy to the municipal councils newly created in the major urban centers—i.e., in nearly all the respective state capitals. This raised the embarrassing future possibility that members of one race or party might govern at state and national levels, while members of another race or party might prevail locally. This would be even more embarrassing if the local council were also the state capital.

Kuala Lumpur

The first elections in Kuala Lumpur are regarded as highly significant by most students of Malaya because of the formation of the Alliance Party (when the MCA and UMNO banded together to contest the 1952 election against Dato Onn bin Ja'afar's IMP). Between 1952 and 1960 Kuala Lumpur was governed by a municipal council, the majority of which was elected. Of the twelve elected councillors, six were Chinese, four were Malay, and two were Indian. This distribution remained intact every year from 1953 until 1958, when one of the elected Malays gave way to an Indian, thus reducing Malay representation on the council. The electoral wards had been drawn in such a way as to ensure these racial distributions: Imbi and Petaling wards each returned three Chinese councillors, Sentul ward three Malays, and Bungsar ward three of either Indian or Malay extraction. Sentul ward is comprised mainly of the district of Kampong Bahru, which is a Malay land reservation in Kuala Lumpur. Non-Malays are not permitted to buy or lease land in this area; hence it was expected that Sentul's representatives would be Malay.

At no time was the Kuala Lumpur Municipal Council a fully elective body. A resolution for a fully elective council for Kuala Lumpur was proposed by councillors Ong Yoke Lin and Abdul Aziz bin Ishak (thereafter the latter never fared well in Alliance politics) and adopted on 31 May 1955. This resolution was subsequently superseded by the adoption of a nonpartisan committee's recommendation that elections be suspended until a decision could be reached about the future status of the council. Beginning 1 November 1959 elections were suspended for twelve months by *Local Authorities Elections (Selangor) Order, 1959*. Twelve months were evidently insufficient to reach agreement, and elections were suspended for an additional six months by order of *Local Authorities Elections (Selangor) Order, 1960*. Eighteen months proved adequate: on 1 April 1961 the *Federal Capital Act no. 35 of 1960* created an appointed commissioner and an advisory staff to replace the previously elective council.

The official argument that the federal capital should be governed as a nonpartisan city was undoubtedly embraced more enthusiastically by Malay residents than by Chinese. There is almost *no* doubt that a fully elective municipal council would have a Chinese majority and that the party affiliation of most of those Chinese would not be MCA. This is not armchair conjecture. In the 1961 and 1962 nationwide local elections, the Chinese won 2,013 seats, Malays won 874, and Indians (and others) about 110. In the 1962 elections alone, roughly 80 percent of the successful candidates were Chinese.[4] Silcock observes that these non-Malay pressures would probably have increased in Kuala Lumpur if it had not been deprived of its elected status. In the absence of the *Federal Capital Act,* Kuala Lumpur would be the seat of a Malay-majority parliamentary government and Chinese-majority (opposition) local council.

Penang

The first elections held in modern Malaya were for seats to the Penang City Council in 1951. Thereafter, annual elections were held for three of the nine elective municipal councillors; the remaining six were appointed. In 1956 the council became fully elective as a result of the *Settlement of Penang Enactments no. 2 and no. 3.* As in Kuala Lumpur, elections were suspended for twelve months in 1959 by order of *Local Authorities Elections (Penang) Order, 1959* and remained suspended for an additional six months beginning 1 October 1960 by authority of *Local Authorities Elections (Penang) Order, 1960.*

Elections were reinstated by the *Local Government Elections Act, 1960,* which repealed the 1950 ordinance, changed the Penang Municipal Council to a city council, and provided for the elections of city councillors within sixty days from 31 March 1969. Under this law, elections were held in 1961 and 1963. Because of the emergency declared during the confrontation with Indonesia, local elections were again suspended in

1964, 1965, and 1966. Penang's history as an elective local body ended in July 1966 when the functions of the city council were taken over by the Penang State Government. At that time state authorities ordered an investigation into the city council's management of affairs, reporting in August 1967 that several councillors were guilty of charges of malpractice and maladministration.

How were state authorities able to take over the management of the Penang City Council, especially in view of the legally designated autonomy of the local body? At first glance the entire procedure seems unconstitutional. But in this instance Parliament moved quickly, passing an act entitled *Malaysia. Local Government Elections (Amendment) (no. 2) Act, 1966,* which was retroactively dated to begin on 26 January 1959. This act gave state legislative assemblies the authority to transfer the functions of municipal (city) councils to the state authorities when the state deemed such a transfer desirable or in the public interest. The Penang State Government followed suit with the *Municipal (Amendment) (Penang) Enactment, 1966,* which specifically authorized the Penang State Government to take over the functions of the city council; if necessary, to hold an inquiry into matters about the council, and to issue further orders as the state deemed fit. A more exact order, the *City Council of George Town (Transfer of Functions) Order, 1966,* transferred all the functions of the council to the chief minister of Penang and created a Commission of Enquiry to look into those council affairs that had occurred since 31 December 1958.

Although the *ex post facto* character of this legal review seems sufficiently obvious, no one challenged the constitutionality of the entire procedure in the courts (because of an alleged shortage of funds). Penang councillors were not the only victims. The functions of the Seremban Town Council (controlled by a non-Alliance coalition) were preempted by the Negri Sembilan State Government, pending an inquiry into maladministration charges against the council. Similarly, the powers of the non-Malay, Labor Party–dominated Malacca Town Council were placed under the Alliance-dominated Malacca State Government.

In 1965 a Royal Commission Enquiry on Local Government Elections was set up and chaired by Senator Athi Nahappan. The commission was supposed to report to Parliament by December 1967, and in the course of its preparation leaders of opposition parties speculated that the report would do away with local elections where non-Malays formed the majority of the electorate. The inquiry was attacked by Mr. D. R. Seenivasagam of the Peoples' Progressive Party, who claimed that the Alliance—which had failed to capture several most important councils, such as Penang, Ipoh, and Seremban by democratic elections—was trying to gain control by "dictatorial methods by doing away with elections." [5]

The Royal Commission finally submitted its report to the Ministry of Local Government and Housing in January 1969; it had taken three years to compile, contained 306 recommendations, and made up fifteen volumes of testimony, evidence, and findings.[6] It was accepted by the National Council on Local Government and was to be made available for inspection to the central state governments by 10 February. Chin Cheng Mei, a *Straits Times* reporter, did not conjecture the likely outcome.

The now notorious race riots following the 13 May 1969 general election interrupted the normal proceedings of parliamentary government that might otherwise have resolved the issue of local elections. But Parliament was reinstated in February 1971, and once again the issue of local elections could be scheduled for resolution. Resolution finally came on 8 July 1971, when Minister of Technology, Research, and Local Government Dato Ong Kee Hui announced that the government had decided to abolish elected local governments. This decision had been made because, in his words, "the government considered elected local governments to be unnecessary and redundant." [7] Since, as he put it, Malaysia is a small country that already has representatives at both national and state levels, the country does not "need" [sic] another tier of representative government at local levels. Malaysia was clearly too small to "need" so much representative government.

Less than a week later, the Mentri Besar of Selangor, Dato Haji Harun, in a debate during the Selangor state legislative session, insisted that "only politicians will clamour for the elected local councils for their own benefits," and, therefore, the Selangor State Government was in the process of degazetting the local councils one by one and taking them over.[8]

On 10 December 1971, a summary version of the Nahappan report was released to the public.[9] By and large, the report favored the reestablishment of local elections. But Dato Ong Kee Hui insisted that the government could not consider local elections until the state governments had restructured their local authorities; the matter, he said, was for the state governments to decide. Meanwhile, the state authorities claimed that they could not reinstitute local elections while they were in the process of changing the boundaries and administrative system of local authorities.[10] Opposition leaders hinted that previously defeated MCA candidates would now be able to get into municipal, town, and local councils "through the back door."

While this entire legal procedure was naively clumsy, we now know how the Penang and other state governments were able to take over the management of the city council. We have not, however, yet established the reason why.

Table 12 shows the racial composition of the Penang City Council from 1951 to 1963, the date of the last-held elections. The extent of Chinese dominance stands out immediately. This was a recent phenomenon in Penang; prior to 1961, no more than seven of the elected councillors were Chinese. Regardless of political party affiliation, the dissolution of the Penang City Council terminated a period of Chinese rule.

Table 12 RACIAL COMPOSITION OF PENANG CITY
COUNCILLORS (ELECTED) FROM 1951
TO 1963, BY FREQUENCIES

Year	Chinese	Malays	Indians	Others
1951	4	1	3	1
1952	3	2	3	1
1953	3	2	3	1
1954	2	4	2	1
1955	2	4	2	1
1956	6	4	5	
1957	7	3	5	
1958	7	4	3	1
1961	12	1	2	
1963	10	3	2	

Sources: Municipality of George Town, Penang, Reports, 1951 to
1956, and *City Council of George Town, Penang, Reports,*
1957 to 1963.

The voting results, as seen in Table 13, show a steady increase in votes received by Chinese candidates relative to the
candidates of other races (not forgetting, of course, the caveats
about the ecological fallacy). The reason for the low Chinese
percentage in 1958 was that several of the five contested
seats were situated in Malay and Indian residential areas.
Though the table does not reveal whether individuals who
crossed racial lines to vote in earlier elections expressed a
racial preference in later contests, it can be seen that Malay
candidates fared less well in the 1960s than in the 1950s.

Who was in power in the Penang State Government during
the legal takeover of the city council's functions?—the Alliance. Alliance members won eighteen of twenty-four contested Penang State Legislative Assembly seats in the 1964
general elections, and—of crucial importance—ten of those
eighteen were Malay. These results placed UMNO members
in a commanding position in Penang state politics, both vis-à-
vis the MCA and the opposition. Though the chief instigators
in the city council suspension cannot be readily identified, the

fact that the Penang Alliance government passed the necessary legislation permitting a takeover of city council functions
indicates that such actions were in the interests of the Penang
State Government. Parliamentary cooperation, as the passage
of the 1966 local governments act clearly shows, also means
that the suspension of Penang's city council was in the interest

Table 13 PENANG CITY COUNCIL ELECTION RESULTS
FOR 1951, 1958, 1961, AND 1963

	1951*	*1958*	*1961*	*1963*
Number of valid votes	22,872	21,040	67,473	65,600
Number of seats	9	5	15	15
Percentage of vote for Chinese candidates	40.9	32.9	75.1	79.6
Percentage of vote for Malay candidates	21.2	26.7	6.4	12.9
Percentage of vote for Indian candidates	34.4	34.6	16.3	7.5
Percentage of vote for Others	3.6	5.8	2.2	0.0

Sources: *Report on the Introduction of Elections in the Municipality
of George Town, Penang, 1951* (Kuala Lumpur: Govern-
ment Press, 1953); *Penang State Gazettes,* 1958, 1961, and
1963.

Note: * The 1951 elections were held with multimember, three-vote
constituencies.

of Alliance rulers at the national level. That the Negri Sembilan takeover of Seremban's local council and Malacca's takeover of the Malacca Town Council both entailed Alliance state
governments and opposition (Chinese-run) local governments
suggests that the recent history of local government in Malaya
is not a matter of pure chance.

My general explanation for the dissolution of elected local
government in Malaya is that national and state Alliance
(chiefly UMNO) governments did not particularly care for the
existence of opposition, chiefly Chinese-run municipal govern-

ments. A second factor, much harder to substantiate, is that UMNO's superiority over the MCA within the framework of the Alliance is better served when the MCA is not too strong. MCA or opposition Chinese-run local councils are not in the long-run interest of the Malay community as defined by UMNO.

This brief review of local elections in modern Malaya suggests that majorities do manipulate electoral rules for partisan advantage. An overview of Malayan politics reveals that urban areas are the only vulnerable constituencies for Malay candidates. These urban constituencies can be offset in state and parliamentary elections by means of gerrymandering and by the fact that Malays constitute a majority of the national population. But at the level of local elections, Chinese voters prefer Chinese officials and have generally tended to vote for their own kind. These observations make it difficult to accept the official position that local politics is no longer elective because of corruption, malpractice, and maladministration (even if the charges are true). Race cannot be discounted as the central ingredient in explaining the changes in local Malayan politics.

STATE AND NATIONAL POLITICS

Nationwide elections were first held in Malaya in 1955. Of the ninety-eight Legislative Council seats, fifty-two were elective; of these, fifty-one were won by the Alliance—a coalition of Malay, Chinese, and Indian racial parties. This election took place during the "preindependence multiracial cooperative" period of Malayan history. A close look at Table 14 reveals how the Kuala Lumpur and Penang urban resident cast his vote. In each case an MCA candidate won easily, testifying that the mood of this pre-*merdeka* (i.e., preindependence) electorate was both moderate and optimistic.

There is, however, one qualifying statistic. The stringent citi-

Table 14   LEGISLATIVE COUNCIL ELECTION
RESULTS (1955) FOR KUALA LUMPUR
AND PENANG CONSTITUENCIES

Kuala Lumpur			
Kuala Lumpur Barat[a]		*Kuala Lumpur Timor*	
Ong Yoke Lin (MCA)[c]	4,667[b]	Cheah Ewe Keat (MCA)	6,790
Abdullah bin Ibrahim (NEG)	1,371	Mohd. Salleh bin Hakin (NEG)	2,431
Tan Tuan Boon (LP)	1,018	Abdul Wahab bin Abdul Majid (IND)	1,003
No. Registered Voters	8,862	No. Registered Voters	13,184

Penang	
George Town	
Chee Swee Ee (MCA)	7,253
Ooi Thiam Siew (LP)	2,650
Cheah Phee Aik (IND)	429
No. Registered Voters	19,935

Source: T. E. Smith, *Report on the First Election of Members to the Legislative Council* (Kuala Lumpur: Government Press, 1955).

Notes: [a] Name of constituency
[b] Number of votes received
[c] Party affiliation is in parentheses. In Tables 14, 15, 16, 17, and 18 the following symbols are used: A—Alliance; MCA—Malayan Chinese Association; MIC—Malayan Indian Congress; UMNO—United Malays National Organization; LP—Labor Party; PR—Party Ra'ayat; IND—Independent; SF—Socialist Front; NEG—Party Negara; PAP—Peoples Action Party; PMIP—Pan Malayan Islamic Party; PPP—Peoples Progressive Party; UDP—United Democratic Party; GRM—Gerakan Ra'ayat Malaysia; DAP—Democratic Action Party.

zenship requirements then in effect made most Chinese ineligible to vote. Of 255,000 persons living in the two Kuala Lumpur constituencies, only 22,000 registered to vote, and of these approximately 64 percent were Malays. Overall, Malays made up 84 percent of the 1955 registered electorate; the Chinese, representing 37 percent of the Malayan population, comprised only 11 percent of the electorate. Relaxed citizenship laws and the coming of age of many Chinese (twenty-one years) had dramatically changed these percentages by 1959. Now 36 percent of the electorate was Chinese—a figure more nearly equal to the Chinese proportion of the nation's population.[11] This suggests that although UMNO was able to marshall its Malay supporters to vote for MCA candidates, there is no corresponding evidence that the MCA was able to do likewise for UMNO.

The electoral history of the Kuala Lumpur and Penang constituencies appears in Tables 15 through 19; though each is treated individually, some general comments apply. First, each table includes (where available) the number of registered electors for every constituency. This is done to illustrate the wide disparities discussed in chapters 2 and 3. In Table 15, for example, Bungsar is nearly double the size of the three remaining Kuala Lumpur constituencies and is substantially in excess of any rural constituency throughout the entire peninsula. Similarly, Table 17 shows how disparate the Selangor State Legislative Assembly constituencies are, ranging from 11,000 to a high of 35,000 (1964 figures). Note that Kampong Bahru, almost entirely Malay, is easily the smallest constituency, whereas Salak, virtually non-Malay, is by far the largest. A resident of Kampong Bahru had three times the voting power of his Salak counterpart. For both the state and parliamentary constituencies, Penang is much more evenly apportioned. Put into a national perspective (for the 1969 elections), the apportionment varied from a low of 17,750 in Ulu Selangor to a high of 81,086 in Bungsar. Though the average constituency ranged around 30,000, the highly urban areas of Penang, Selangor, and Malacca averaged closer to 47,000. Here, to the disadvantage of the Chinese, the principle of equal representation is severely distorted.*

* For another discussion on constituency delimitation, see Jean Grossholtz, "Integrative Factors in the Malaysian and Phillipine Legislatures," *Comparative Politics* 3, no. 1 (October 1970):97–99.

Each table documents in miniature my characterization of Malayan racial politics (see chapter 3): the postindependence racial cooperation, the growing salience of race, and, finally, the demise of moderation accompanied by the decline of the multiracial coalition. MCA candidates fared much better in 1959 than in 1969 when they lost badly to the less moderate parties that championed Chinese interests.

Finally, the three- and four-cornered contests that characterized the 1964 election gave way to straight two-way fights between the MCA and either Gerakan or the DAP following a no-contest agreement among the opposition parties. The tables are self-evident in this respect.

Kuala Lumpur (Parliamentary) Constituencies[12]

What is immediately apparent in Table 15 is the brilliant success of DAP and Gerakan candidates against the MCA in 1969—these have been starred for easy reading. In only one constituency—Setapak—did the MCA have even a chance. It was beaten badly in the other three by margins ranging from two-to-one to four-to-one—in short, by landslide proportions. MCA candidates had won one of the four seats in 1959 and added another in 1964. The 1969 outcome must have come as something of a shock. Tan Toh Hong, an easy winner in 1964, was overwhelmed in 1969. The MCA seat in Setapak also disappeared in the avalanche. The credibility of the MCA clearly suffered an enormous gap in 1969.

Penang (Parliamentary) Constituencies

From Table 16 it is clear that Penang has never been an MCA stronghold. MCA politicians have never won a parlimentary seat in Penang, although several of them performed respectably in 1959 and 1964. But in 1969 these MCA candi-

Table 15   PARLIAMENTARY ELECTION RESULTS FOR KUALA LUMPUR CONSTITUENCIES FOR THE 1959, 1964, AND 1969 ELECTIONS

1959

Batu

Ng Ann Teck (LP)	8,737
Lim Hee Hong (MCA)	6,408
No. Reg'd Voters	20,819

Bungsar

Ong Yeow Kay (PPP)	2,388
V. David (LP)	9,734
Koh Pooi Kee (IND)	6,821
Kaw Joo Kooi (MCA)	5,036
No. Reg'd Voters	35,549

Bukit Bintang

Heng Cheng Swee (IND)	270
Robert Hoh (IND)	5,434
Nazar Nong (PR)	4,593
Cheah Theam Swee (MCA)	6,134
No. Reg'd Voters	24,984

Setapak

A. Boestaman (PR)	6,901
Yap Kim Swee (IND)	3,853
Aisah Ghani (UMNO)	4,805
No. Reg'd Voters	22,490

1964

Batu

Too Chee Cheong (PAP)	2,459
Yap Chin Kwee (MCA)	9,774
Tan Chee Khoon (LP)	10,122
No. Reg'd Voters	32,297

Bungsar

Devan Nair (PAP)	13,494
Chew Choo Soot (PPP)	2,219
Koh Pooi Kee (MCA)	9,761
V. David (LP)	12,686
No. Reg'd Voters	58,261

Bukit Bintang

Tan Toh Hong (MCA)	9,107
Abdul A. Ismail (PMIP)	650
Ishak B. Haji Mhd. (PR)	5,000
Wong Lin Ken (PAP)	6,667
No. Reg'd Voters	33,636

Setapak

K.V. Thaver (PAP)	4,214
Tajuddin Kahar (PR)	7,888
S.Y. Chan (MCA)	12,292
No. Reg'd Voters	37,034

1969

Batu

Tan Chee Khoon (GRM)	22,720*
Yap Chin Kwee (MCA)	8,772

Bungsar

Goh Hock Guan (DAP)	37,050*
Lew Sip Hon (MCA)	9,648

Bukit Bintang

Yeoh Teck Chye (GRM)	18,488*
Tan Toh Hong (MCA)	9,137

Setapak

Walter Loh (DAP)	17,137*
Teh Hock Heng (MCA)	13,871

Sources: Election Commission. *Report on the Parliamentary and State Elections, 1959* (Kuala Lumpur: Government Press, 1960); Election Commission. *Report on the Parliamentary (Dewan Ra'ayat) and State Legislative Assembly General Elections, 1964, of the States of Malaya* (Kuala Lumpur: Government Press, 1965); *Straits Times*, 12 May 1969.

Notes: * Indicates winner in the 1969 Elections.

dates obtained less than 20 percent of the combined vote in the Tanjong and Dato Kramat constituencies.

Kuala Lumpur (Selangor State Legislative Assembly) Constituencies

The legal boundaries of Kuala Lumpur and the State Legislative Assembly constituencies do not overlap perfectly. Selected here are the six constituencies that best represent the voting behavior of the Kuala Lumpur electorate. In Table 17 one pattern is pronounced: the steady deterioration of the MCA. Having held three state seats in 1959, the MCA lost one in 1964 and the remaining two in 1969. The party took a terrible beating in each contest, losing chiefly to the more extremist DAP in 1969. The MCA did so poorly in 1969 that for the first time since independence, the Alliance Party no longer held a majority in the Selangor State Government.

Penang (Penang State Legislative Assembly) Constituencies

As might have been predicted from Table 16, the position of the MCA in Penang state politics would most likely be very tenuous. Of the nine designated urban constituencies, only one was ever won by an MCA candidate (he obtained the Kelawei seat in 1959 and 1964). However, he too fell victim to the extremist pressures that dominated parliamentary and state elections in 1969. The margins of victory for Gerakan and DAP candidates in Penang in 1969 are almost unreal, ranging anywhere from double to sixfold the MCA totals. The election gave the Penang State Government to Gerakan, and Lim Chong Eu became Penang's chief minister. These results differ dramatically from those in Table 14, where the moderate MCA had done so well.

Table 16   PARLIAMENTARY ELECTION RESULTS FOR PENANG
CONSTITUENCIES FOR THE 1959, 1964, AND 1969 ELECTIONS

1959		1964		1969	
Tanjong		*Tanjong*		*Tanjong*	
Khoo Yat See (PPP)	2,107	Lim Chong Eu (UDP)	12,928	Lim Chong Eu (GRM)	19,656*
Goh Guan Ho (MCA)	6,448	Tan Chong Bee (PAP)	778	Chuah Teng Siew (MCA)	4,496
Tan Phock Kin (LP)	11,333	Choong Ewe Leong (MCA)	6,271	Khoo Yat See (PPP)	775
		Tan Phock Kin (LP)	8,516		
No. Reg'd Voters	28,086	No. Reg'd Voters	34,763		
Dato Kramat		*Dato Kramat*		*Dato Kramat*	
Lee Thean-Chu (MCA)	5,048	Lim Cheng Poh (MCA)	7,707	V. David (GRM)	17,272*
Lim Kean Siew (LP)	10,474	Teh Ewe Lim (UDP)	8,236	Lim Chong Hai (MCA)	5,635
C.M. Ramli (IND)	286	Lim Kean Siew (LP)	10,102		
No. Reg'd Voters	22,058	No. Reg'd Voters	31,327		

Sources: See Table 15.
Notes: See Tables 14 and 15.

Table 17

STATE ELECTION RESULTS FOR KUALA LUMPUR
CONSTITUENCIES FOR THE 1959, 1964, AND 1969 ELECTIONS

1959		*1964*		*1969*	
Penchala		*Penchala*		*Penchala*	
Y.P. Liu (LP)	2,133	Ng Ann Teck (LP)	2,894	Hor Cheok (DAP)	8,389*
Lim Jew Siang (MCA)	2,299	Lim Jew Siang (MCA)	3,065	Lim Jew Siang (MCA)	2,735
		Too Chee Cheong (PAP)	1,409		
No. Reg'd Voters	7,291	No. Reg'd Voters	11,986		
Pantai		*Pantai*		*Pantai*	
Teh Hung Kiat (MCA)	4,105	Goh Hock Guan (PAP)	3,958	V. David (GRM)	16,117*
R. Madhavan (PPP)	82	Cheong Thiam Leong (PPP)	352	C.K. Cheah (MCA)	6,088
V. David (LP)	4,295	Seow Yu Boon (MCA)	5,341		
		V. David (LP)	5,701		
No. Reg'd Voters	13,105	No. Reg'd Voters	23,038		
Salak		*Salak*		*Salak*	
Douglas K.K. Lee (MCA)	6,291	Woo Hon Kong (LP)	9,202	Goh Hock Guan (DAP)	20,335*
Kong Chee Ken (LP)	409	Chew Choo Soot (PPP)	5,658	Seow Yu Boon (MCA)	4,141
Chew Choo Soot (PPP)	4,059	Goh Keng Fook (MCA)	7,616		
Koh Pooi Kee (IND)	4,304				
No. Reg'd Voters	22,432	No. Reg'd Voters	35,223		

Bukit Nanas		Bukit Nanas		Bukit Nanas	
Lee Yoon Thim (MCA)	4,749	Loong Foong Beng (MCA)	5,691	Lee Lam Thye (DAP)	13,275*
Americk Singh Gill (LP)	4,150	Lau Kit Sun (PAP)	5,117	Loong Foong Beng (MCA)	4,590
		Gan Yong Ming (LP)	3,641		
No. Reg'd Voters	15,519	No. Reg'd Voters	22,480		
Kampong Bahru		*Kampong Bahru*		*Kampong Bahru*	
Abdullah Yassin (UMNO)	2,703	Abdullah Yassin (UMNO)	4,448	Haji Ahmad Razli (UMNO)	3,805*
Kamarudin bin Abu Hassan (PR)	1,447	Ishak bin Haji Mohammad (PR)	2,191	Mohamed bin Mohamed Soom (GRM)	3,552
Syed Ibrahim bin Syed Salim (PAS)	1,086	Syed Ibrahim bin Syed Salim (IND)	195	Muhammed bin Haniff (PMIP)	1,696
No. Reg'd Voters	9,475	No. Reg'd Voters	11,156		
Sentul		*Sentul*		*Sentul*	
Abdul Aziz b. Is. (PAS)	848	K.V. Thaver (PAP)	1,559	Lee Beng Cheng (DAP)	8,424*
Devaki Krishnan (MIC)	2,413	P.T. Arasu (MIC)	5,674	P.T. Arasu (MIC)	5,242
Nazar Nong (PR)	2,965	P.G. Lim (LP)	4,231		
No. Reg'd Voters	11,999	No. Reg'd Voters	17,856		

Source: See Table 15.
Notes: See Tables 14 and 15.

Table 18   STATE ELECTION RESULTS FOR PENANG CONSTITUENCIES
                 FOR THE 1959, 1964, AND 1969 ELECTIONS

1959		*1964*		*1969*	
Kota		*Kota*		*Kota*	
Lee Kok Liang (LP)	3,453	Lim Chong Eu (UDP)	4,065	Lim Chong Eu (GRM)	6,038*
Lee Thean-Chu (MCA)	2,255	Lim Ewe Hock (PAP)	165	Khaw Kok Chwee (MCA)	1,443
Jaswant Singh (PPP)	379	Liang Juen Chew (MCA)	1,962	Khoo Yat See (PPP)	262
Choong Han Leong (IND)	74	Tan Puah Kim (LP)	2,937		
No. Reg'd Voters	8,712	No. Reg'd Voters	11,375		
Tanjong Tengah		*Tanjong Tengah*		*Tanjong Tengah*	
Wong Choon Woh (LP)	3,742	Teh Geok Kooi (UDP)	4,055	Tan Gin Hwa (GRM)	7,435*
Sam Ah Chow (MCA)	2,736	Kang Eng Wah (PAP)	359	Ma Cheok Tat (MCA)	1,889
Khoo Yat See (PPP)	1,208	Lee Woon Mun (MCA)	2,401	Teh Geok Kooi (PPP)	320
		Wong Choong Woh (LP)	3,576		
No. Reg'd Voters	10,413	No. Reg'd Voters	13,018		
Dhoby Ghaut		*Dhoby Ghaut*		*Dhoby Ghaut*	
Mohamed Ismal bin Che Din (UMNO)		Khoo Yat See (PPP)	670	Khoo Teng Chye (GRM)	6,882*
Uncontested		M.S.A. Zachariah (A)	4,179	S.M. Mohd. Idris (UMNO)	2,959
		Cheah Cheng Keat (UDP)	1,773		
		Arshad Yusoff (PR)	2,113		
		No. Reg'd Voters	10,714		

Tanjong Utara

Yuen Fook Cheong (LP) — 3,124
M.S.A. Zachariah (A) — 1,938
Lim Cheng Poh (PPP) — 999
Wong Loh Hun (IND) — 430
No. Reg'd Voters — 8,953

Tanjong Barat

Tan Chong Bee (LP) — 2,053
Hwant Yang Chou (MCA) — 1,643
Jag-Jit Singh (PPP) — 1,229
No. Reg'd Voters — 6,687

Sungei Pinang

D.S. Ramanathan (LP) — 2,991
P.W. David (MIC) — 1,702
Abdul Jalil bin Shaik Mohamed (NEG) — 643
No. Reg'd Voters — 7,668

*Tanjong **Selatan*

C.Y. Choy (LP) — 4,271
Foo Yew Fong (MCA) — 1,290
Lim Book Phoon (PPP) — 379
No. Reg'd Voters — 7,703

Tanjong Utara

Khoo Kay Por (UDP) — 2,877
Tan Chong Bee (PAP) — 535
Choong Ewe Leong (MCA) — 2,571
Loh Guan Kheng (LP) — 2,656
No. Reg'd Voters — 10,370

Tanjong Barat

C.Y. Choy (LP) — 2,470
Cheah Hock Seng (MCA) — 2,052
Teh Ewe Lim (UDP) — 3,610
No. Reg'd Voters — 9,730

Sungei Pinang

Lee Sinn Boon (UDP) — 1,385
Omar b. Othman (PR) — 3,120
D.S. Ramanathan (MIC) — 4,236
No. Reg'd Voters — 10,717

Tanjong Selatan

Teh Poh Hua (MCA) — 1,376
Khor Peng Seat (LP) — 4,789
Loh Lian Kee (UDP) — 3,066
No. Reg'd Voters — 10,880

Tanjong Utara

Khoo Kay Por (GRM) — 5,878*
Lam Wu Chong (MCA) — 1,568
Cheah Cheng Keat (PPP) — 161

Tanjong Barat

Teh Ewe Lim (GRM) — 5,879*
Oon Hoot Ewe (MCA) — 1,044

Sungei Pinang

Chellian s/o Poosony (GRM) — 5,099*
Amaladass Ponnusamy (MIC) — 3,325

Tanjong Selatan

Wong Choong Woh (GRM) — 6,341*
Teh Cheng Lim (MCA) — 1,099

Table 18   STATE ELECTION RESULTS FOR PENANG CONSTITUENCIES
FOR THE 1959, 1964, AND 1969 ELECTIONS (*Continued*)

1959		1964		1969	
Kelawei		*Kelawei*		*Kelawei*	
Tan Khim Hoe (MCA)	1,382	Triptial Singh (LP)	1,324	Yeap Ghim Guan (DAP)	4,239*
Oh Cheow Hong (PPP)	601	Lim Hean Chie (UDP)	1,497	Tan Khim Hoe (MCA)	1,850
Oliver Phipps (IND)	535	Tan Khim Hoe (MCA)	2,658		
A. Raja Gopal (IND)	171				
Syed Salleh Alsagoff (NEG)					
No. Reg'd Voters	4,471	No. Reg'd Voters	6,818		
Jelutong		*Jelutong*		*Jelutong*	
Ooi Thiam Siew (LP)	4,612	Chang Lai Sum (UDP)	2,552	Koay Boon Seng (DAP)	8,242*
Lim Eng Hooi	2,196	Khaw Kok Chwee (MCA)	3,159	Choong Teik Seng (MCA)	3,232
M. Abraham (PPP)	420	Tan Hock Hin (LP)	4,999		
Zakaria bin Shaik Abdul Aziz (PAS)	450				
No. Reg'd Voters	10,514	No. Reg'd Voters	13,057		

Sources: See Table 15.
Notes: See Tables 14 and 15.

This is essentially a trend analysis for selected constituencies. The analysis shows the increasing success of racial extremism and the decline of moderation (as represented by the MCA). Though the tables do not indicate which of the urban voters switched from the moderate MCA to more extremist DAP, UDP, GRM, and Labor Party candidates, nor what their social, economic, or educational background might be, it is evident that a switch occurred. A similar constituency-by-constituency analysis for the rest of Malaya would show that the moderate Alliance in general fared worse in 1969 than ever before.

A review of the chapter to this point suggests: (1) Chinese (chiefly opposition party) domination of municipal councils, leading to their abolition, and (2) Chinese (opposition party) command of the urban constituencies that make up Kuala Lumpur and Penang representation in both national and state government. Returning to the survey respondents, whose opinions were recorded in February and March of 1967, it will be seen that the 1969 results could have been predicted for the urban constituencies discussed.

POLITICAL PREFERENCE

The survey sought answers to four specific questions: (1) extent of voter registration, (2) actual turnout (participation), (3) party affiliation, and (4) party preference.

Malay registration in both cities was higher than Chinese. In Kuala Lumpur, 50 percent of the Malays interviewed said they were registered to vote, compared with 44 percent for the Chinese. The corresponding percentages for Penang are 67 and 56.* Asked whether they had voted within the past three years in any election (the relevant election is the 1964 general parliamentary and state election), Kuala Lumpur respondents dis-

---

* These percentages would be uniformly increased by about one-fifth if underage respondents were deleted from the analysis.

play percentages of 31 (Malay) and 36 (Chinese), the corresponding figures for Penang being 62 and 39 percent respectively.

Chinese turnout in the two cities has been analyzed elsewhere in an attempt to determine the effect that differences in education, age, sex, and religion had on the extent of turnout.* It was learned that neither sex nor religion makes any difference and that middle-aged Chinese vote more than either the young or very old (as expected). Curiously enough, when education was plotted against voter turnout, it was discovered that turnout declined with higher levels of learning. In both cities the illiterate or poorly educated Chinese voted at double to triple the rate of those who had completed all or some of secondary school.** This result runs counter to the general norm in most Western industrial societies, where higher education increases political participation. The explanation may be that better educated urban Chinese are more alienated from politics than those less educated and are less interested in doing their citizen duty, or that the poorly educated were better organized and mobilized to turn out at the polls. (It would be extremely interesting to do this same analysis for the 1969 general elections.)

Asked about active party membership, 19 percent of the Malay respondents in Kuala Lumpur and 29 percent in Penang stated they were active members of a political party—nearly all belonged to UMNO. Of the Chinese, about 1 percent—three persons in Kuala Lumpur and two in Penang—claimed party membership. These figures are suspiciously low, but it is

* See Alvin Rabushka, "A Note on Overseas Chinese Political Participation in Urban Malaya," *American Political Science Review* 64, no. 1 (March 1970):177–78.

** Although the number of Malay respondents is too small to permit any such statistically meaningful controls as the one relating education to participation for Chinese, I nonetheless ran the Malay data cards through the counter-sorter and, unexpectedly, the same pattern appeared—better educated Malays did not vote to the same degree as poorly educated ones.

difficult to obtain accurate membership statistics for parties.
Party officials politely refused these numbers or promised they
would be mailed to me in some ambiguous future. Thus although I can do no better than *face validity* for this question,
it is almost certain that the Chinese held back in their responses.

Table 19 PARTY PREFERENCES BY PERCENTAGES

	Kuala Lumpur	
	(N = 48)	(N = 269)
Party	Malays	Chinese
United Malays National Organization	100.0	
Malayan Chinese Association		26.8
Democratic Action Party		10.0
Labor Party		4.8
No Response		56.5
	Penang	
	(N = 63)	(N = 252)
Party	Malays	Chinese
United Malays National Organization	84.1	
Malayan Chinese Association		14.7
Labor Party		4.8
United Democratic Party		1.6
No Response	11.1	77.4

The most interesting and useful information obtained in the
political portion of the survey came in response to the question: "Which party do you think would do the best job in government?" The results appear in Table 19. Malay support for
UMNO is unquestioned. Chinese support for the MCA is another matter. About 27 percent of the Kuala Lumpur Chinese
seem to be MCA supporters and about half that number in
Penang. How do these percentages compare with the actual
voting in 1969?

Tables 15 and 16 enable us to compute the actual vote percentages obtained by MCA candidates in the parliamentary elections for the two cities. MCA candidates in Kuala Lumpur received about 30 percent of the vote; in Penang, about 21 percent. Setting aside caveats about ecological fallacies for the moment, these percentages are very close to the party preferences expressed by the survey respondents. Certainly the percentages are close enough to have told the MCA what to have expected prior to the 1969 election.

Little more needs to be said about the desirability and feasibility of survey research in Malaya's multiracial society. An objection might be raised to the large "no response" category for Chinese in Table 19, but if we construe these as nongovernment supporters, our interpretation makes sense. As Ratnam and Milne suggested in their study of the 1964 election, most opponents of government would probably remain silent when asked their party preference. Silence is here equivalent to opposition support, and the voting results support that inference.

The relationship between racial tolerance and political participation and preferences was carefully examined as part of the analysis for this book. Chinese respondents were divided into a tolerant-nontolerant dichotomy, and then the extent of voter registration, turnout, party membership, and willingness to express a party preference were examined. No consistent pattern could be found among these items. There was absolutely no difference in the extent of voter registration in Penang, contradictory patterns for Malays and Chinese in Kuala Lumpur, and in general no systematic connection between being tolerant (or nontolerant) and politically active or vocal. Most of those expressing a specific party preference tended to be highly educated but no more or less racially tolerant than those not responding on party preference.

SUMMARY

One of the distinguishing features of this book is its intensive exploration of the city as a microcosm of Malaya's multiracialism. What makes this urban exploration so interesting is that the racial character of the city differs from that of the rural areas and the nation as a whole: the cities are heavily Chinese, while the nation and rural areas are majority Malay. Thus we have considered the racial behavior and values, as well as the political behavior and beliefs, of the minority Chinese community in its urban setting.

Most Chinese will react strongly to the two major themes developed here. The first documented how the Chinese, having won legitimate control of Malaya's major municipal councils, saw their extensive lawful participation in the urban political life of the nation taken from them. Corruption, malpractice, and maladministration are not limited to elected *local* officials. The second combined survey data with trend analysis of parliamentary and state election results to conclude that the moderate position of the MCA was no longer tenable under growing extremist pressures (given the salience of race). The survey statistics correspond very closely to the statistics of the election reports as published by the election commission and the newspapers. Although the constituencies discussed in this chapter do not reflect the rural and more racially balanced areas, they nonetheless support the logical view of racial competition I set forth earlier. The Chinese no longer votes for his municipal (or "city") officers, nor does his vote count equally with those of his Malay countrymen when he votes in federal and state elections.

— 6 —

Conclusion

Must Malayans look forward to a future of increasing conflict? There is little likelihood that democracy can be restored or a free-market economy maintained, and a careful examination of only two urban areas shows how racial pressures can build up, as well as how dominant political communities are likely to react. That is not, however, the entire story. Between Chinese and Malays there exists a substantial reservoir of interracial tolerance (though 13 May may have strained that tolerance in Kuala Lumpur). Survey research reveals that racial stereotypes affect social and political behavior very little and that a good deal of interracial social acceptance can exist in spite of a steadily worsening political situation caused by intensified racial extremism. In other words, racial values, beliefs, and patterns of social behavior are relatively independent of politics.

RACE RELATIONS: A THEORY*

Furnivall initiated the serious study of plural societies in the 1930s. Although thirty years of scholarship has brought a

* I use the tools of modern welfare economics to explore the logic of racial harmony and conflict in another study entitled *A Theory of Racial Harmony* (forthcoming). There the reader can find a more formal treatment of the version given here in chapter 6.

voluminous literature into the field, much of it has been wrong, in the author's opinion, because it has neglected Furnivall's thesis that the races can peacefully meet *only* in the marketplace, buying and selling. According to Furnivall, each race in a plural society will attempt to impose its own values over all the others; hence, plural societies incline toward conflict. Conflict could only be avoided by maintaining colonial rule and a *laissez-faire exchange market economy*.

Several explanations may be advanced to suggest why this point has been overlooked for so long. First, postwar intellectuals, in Britain and in the colonies, no longer supported the empire or colonial rule, as the swift dissolution of the British, Belgian, French, and Dutch colonial empires attests. Secondly, in the interests of nation building, most analysts (and political leaders as well) emphasized the common features and bonds of citizens in plural societies and overlooked their differences. Those who believed that mankind was entering a new era in which centuries of independent cultural and political development could be erased overnight were mistaken.[1]

A third reason is that most analysts of plural societies were sociologists, anthropologists, and political scientists; the number of economists who have applied their skills to the analysis of plural societies is very few.[2] As a result, market exchange in plural societies has received less attention than such topics as kinship practices, social stratification, cultural practices, education, political parties, bureaucracies, and so forth.

That political polarization and social behavior (with its accompanying racial attitudes) are independent of one another has been discovered elsewhere—in, for example, Robert Kearney's description of Ceylon.

The seeming paradox has existed of amicable relations among members of different communities, readily observable at the lowest levels of interaction in the everyday lives of ordinary Ceylonese, at the same time that the communities appear to be locked in mortal struggle in the political sphere.[3]

Again: "Communal competition appeared with the development of the political process and threatened to corrode the tolerant, if not intimate, social relationships which existed between communities." [4]

Ivar Oxaal discovered that a breakdown of the color bar in Trinidad's social life was accompanied by a growing political polarization between Blacks and East Indians.[5]

If we can separate the political and nonpolitical aspects of life in the plural society and understand how this is done, we can understand the results of this book and those of Kearney and Oxaal as well. Market exchange is voluntary exchange and requires agreement between the partners to the exchange. Hence marketplace transactions involve a unanimous, voluntary relationship between buyer and seller, subject, of course, to scarcity. Under these conditions, racial tensions and conflict are minimized. Individuals, as members of specific racial groups, may gain or lose on the basis of their marginal value of productivity (which may be conditioned by genetic, historical, or cultural factors). Groups of individuals having low marginal values of productivity attempt to compensate by seizing public control over resources, i.e., holding political power and the decision-making authority to allocate.

The public activities of government in the multiracial environment thus convert private economic conflict among individuals in markets into group conflict between races. When the economic well-being of groups is significantly affected by political activity, politics becomes a fight between groups (or races) for survival. Thus, in a society in which race is politically crucial, the greater the public use of resources (i.e., the greater the extent of government economic activity), the greater the likelihood of racial conflict. Politics therefore entails neither unanimity nor voluntarism. Dictators or elected majorities can impose universally binding decisions on all the citizenry, including those who do not like the decision. Moreover, the decision may be enforced by coercion—the power of the state. In short, while racial harmony can exist in the marketplace, politics sets race against race in a struggle that is very often to the death.*

FINDINGS

1. Although social and/or cultural unity is neither a necessary nor sufficient condition for political unity, government intervention in a community's cultural affairs may well lead to political turmoil.

2. Majorities often alter the rules of politics to suit their own ends. In Malaya this is illustrated by the dissolution of locally elected councils, constituency delimitation in favor of Malay rural areas, the control exercised over voluntary organizations, the disproportionate disbursements of public revenues (public goods monies) for Malays, and so forth.

3. Democracy is not easy to maintain in Malaya. States of emergency have been in effect from 1948 to 1960, 1963 to 1965, and 1969 to 1971, during which periods constitutional guarantees of individual liberties have been suspended.

4. Multiracial living experiences do not necessarily promote racial tolerance or political unity.

5. Although higher levels of education may promote racial tolerance, they do not ensure political unity or democratic stability.

* The brevity of this account may trouble readers who believe that Malaya's problem of racial discord stems from Malays having to do business with Chinese who dominate the free-market economy. But is free market entry restricted for Malays? My other essay, *A Theory of Racial Harmony*, shows that a free-market economy may be possible only in multiracial societies where the ruling political majority also happens to have, as a community of individuals, relatively high marginal values of productivity. This is the case in Singapore and in the few remaining multiracial British colonies—Gibraltar, Bermuda, and the Bahamas.

Racial harmony is thus more likely to be furthered by reducing the role of government in Malayan society and by
greater reliance on an expanding private sector. It has been
seen, however, that the UMNO government has introduced a
New Economic Policy, which entails a growing role for government in economic activities because of ever-increasing
Malay political pressures. That Malays can be persuaded that
their own self-interest lies in the workings of a laissez-faire
free-market economy is doubtful.

This view is shared by Milton J. Esman, a former adviser
to the Department of the Prime Minister.

> If economic growth and efficient resource use were the
> only goals, Chinese through free competition would success-
> fully dominate virtually all the resources and opportunities at
> the disposal of Malaysian society. Under present conditions
> they can use resources more efficiently, not as a community
> but as individuals and firms. They would also claim an even
> greater proportion of university places and civil service posi-
> tions, but this would be intolerable to the Malays who feel
> they never had a fair chance. And the Malays control gov-
> ernment. If a choice must be made, Malays to a man are
> more interested in reducing through institutional changes the
> present socioeconomic dualism, which so closely matches
> communal lines, than in overall economic growth. . . .[6]

There may well be a more practicable solution, but it
would involve the dissolution of open, competitive party politics in which racial issues can be raised and promoted. The
Malayan government may, in fact, have recognized this in its
promulgation of the 1971 constitutional amendment and
1969 revision of the sedition act which together preclude the
raising of racial issues in politics. The only cause for worry
might lie in a growing terrorist movement that feeds upon the
disillusionment of the unemployed, Chinese-educated urban
proletarian. This will not be a problem if the government can
maintain law and order.

The recent political history of Malaya and Singapore provides an appropriate note on which to conclude this book. Malaya received its independence in 1957. In August 1963 it was joined in a "greater Malaysia" that included Singapore and the former British Borneo territories of Sabah and Sarawak. This union was short-lived. Malaya and Singapore parted company in August 1965 due to a growing Malay fear that Singapore's ambitious Prime Minister Lee Kuan-yew sought to increase Chinese control over the public sector. Given Chinese predominance in the private sector, these ambitions were totally unacceptable to Malay leaders; Singapore, whose population of two million is three-fourths Chinese, was thus expelled from "Malaysia" and forced to declare itself as an independent republic.

Initial fears that Singapore would be unable to survive economically, with its limited land and other resources and its high population density, were unfounded. Singapore's growth rate and per capita incomes *for all races* exceed those of Malaya. It is more to the present purpose to note that relations between Singapore and Malaya have steadily improved since the separation and that the basis of these improved relations is entirely economic: trade between the two countries is voluntary market exchange. Previous fear of racial political competition had strained Chinese-Malay race relations. The separation of coercive politics from markets has led to renewed cooperation. Political competition between Chinese and Malays in a union of Malaya and Singapore had brought the racial situation to an intolerable tension; the separation has permitted economic motives to prevail and relations between the two countries to improve.

Appendix 1

J. 410 Questionnaire

Area Code	J. 410	1–3
1 2 3 4 5 6 7 8 9 0 x y (5)	Georgetown 1	4
1 2 3 4 5 6 7 8 9 0 x y (6)	Kuala Lumpur 2	
	Q'aire No.	(7–9)
	Card 1	(10)

February 1967

Good morning/afternoon/evening. I am an interviewer for SRM. This is a private Company which carries out market research all over Malaya. This week we are conducting a survey of people's habits and general opinions. I would be very grateful for your help.

1. Do you have any of the following things in your household? (READ OUT)

	Yes	No	
Motorbike or scooter	1	2	(11)
Car	1	2	(12)
Rediffusion	1	2	(13)
Radio	1	2	(14)
Telephone	1	2	(15)
Television	1	2	(16)

2(a) Do you ever listen to the radio or not?

Yes	1		(17)
No	2	(GO TO Q. 3)	

105

SHOW CARD 1 (ORANGE)
(b) Here is a number of different kinds of radio programmes.
Would you tell me which type is your favourite?

	(18)	(19)
Variety shows and comedy	1	1
Plays and stories	2	2
Request programmes	3	3
Competitions and Quizzes	4	4
The news	5	5
Religious programmes	6	6
Chinese music and songs	7	7
Malay music and songs	8	8
Indian music and songs	9	9
Western popular music	0	0
Sports commentaries	x	x
(N.R.)	y	y

3(a) Do you ever read newspapers or not?

Yes   1
No   2   (GO TO Q. 3(c))   (20)

     IF YES
(b) What is the name of your favourite newspaper?

....
....
1 2 3 4 5 6 7 8 9 0 x y   (21)
1 2 3 4 5 6 7 8 9 0 x y   (22)

(c) Do you ever read magazines or not?

Yes   1   (23)
No   2 (GO TO Q. 4)

     IF YES
(d) What is the name of your favourite magazine? What type
of magazine is this?
(WRITE IN NAME AND TYPE)
    (NAME) .... (TYPE) ....
....
1 2 3 4 5 6 7 8 9 0 x y   (24)
1 2 3 4 5 6 7 8 9 0 x y   (25)

4(a) Do you ever go to the cinema or not?

Yes	1	(26)
No	2 (GO TO Q. 5)	

IF YES

(b) About how often do you go to the cinema?

Twice a week or more	1	(27)
About once a week	2	
About once in 2 weeks	3	
About once a month	4	
Less often	5	
(D.K./N.R.)	9	

5(a) Where do you have most of your meals?

At own home	1	(28)
At home of close relatives	2	
At friend's home	3	
At restaurants	4	

Others (write in) . . . .

(b) What is your favourite type of restaurant?

Chinese	1	(29)
Malay	2	
Tamil	3	
Indian-Muslim	4	
Chinese-Muslim	5	

Others (write in) . . . .
(N.R.)   9

6(a) Are you a member of any organisation or society such as a Labour Union, club, business association, religious association or co-operative society?

Yes	1	(30)
No	2 (GO TO Q. 7)	

(b) Would you name the organisations or societies you belong to? (FULL NAME AND KIND OF ORGANISATION)

FOR EACH ORGANISATION OR SOCIETY ASK
(c) In . . . . (society) are you an ordinary member or do you hold an office?

(b)	(c)	
Name of Organisation What kind	Ordinary member (Tick)	Title of office (write in)
. . . .	. . . .	
. . . .	. . . .	
. . . .	. . . .	
. . . .	. . . .	
. . . .	. . . .	

OFFICE USE ONLY

No. of organisations	1 2 3 4 5 6 7 8 9 0 x y	(31)
No. of offices	1 2 3 4 5 6 7 8 9 0 x y	(32)
Type of organisation	1 2 3 4 5 6 7 8 9 0 x y	(33)
	1 2 3 4 5 6 7 8 9 0 x y	(34)
	1 2 3 4 5 6 7 8 9 0 x y	(35)

7. What means of transportation do you use *most often* in your daily life?

Car	1	(36)
Taxi	2	
Bus	3	
Motorbike or scooter	4	
Bicycle	5	
Walk	6	
(D.K./N.R.)	9	

8. How often do you travel outstation, that is outside Kuala Lumpur/Georgetown to other towns and the countryside?

Several times a week	1	(37)
Once a week	2	
Once in 2 weeks	3	
Once a month	4	
Once in 3 months	5	
Once in 6 months	6	
Once a year	7	
Less often	8	
(D.K./N.R.)	9	

9. Outside of your immediate family, what types of people do you normally mix with? (IF 'Everyone' or 'everybody' PROBE FOR COMBINATIONS)

Malays	1	(38)
Chinese	2	
Indians	3	
Eurasians	4	
European	5	
Others (write in combinations)		

. . . .

(N.R.)   9

OFFICE USE

COMBINATIONS

1 2 3 4 5 6 7 8 9 0 x y (39)

---

10. Some people say that one way of life is superior to another. Others say there is little difference. In your opinion which way of life do you consider the best? (PROBE FOR COMBINATIONS)

Malay way of life	1	(40)
Chinese way of life	2	
Indian way of life	3	
Western or European way of life	4	
Others (write in)		

. . . .

(N.R.)   9

SHOW CARD II (GREY)

11. I am going to mention some human qualities one at a time. Tell me frankly (PAUSE) what you think.

First, take *AMBITION*. Do you think that among the Chinese their amount of *ambition* is very high, high, low or very low? How about the Malays? How about the Indians?

Now take *ACTIVITY IN PUBLIC AND SOCIAL AFFAIRS*

(ASK FOR EACH RACE. THEN GO ON TO NEXT QUAL-
ITY.)

	CHINESE	MALAYS	INDIANS
AMBITION	(41)	(42)	(43)
	1....Very high	1....Very high	1....Very high
	2....High	2....High	2....High
	3....Low	3....Low	3....Low
	4....Very low	4....Very low	4....Very low
	9....(N.R.)	9....(N.R.)	9....(N.R.)
	5..neither(vol.)	5..neither(vol.)	5..neither(vol.)
ACTIVITY IN PUBLIC AND SOCIAL AFFAIRS	(44)	(45)	(46)
	1....Very high	1....Very high	1....Very high
	2....High	2....High	2....High
	3....Low	3....Low	3....Low
	4....Very low	4....Very low	4....Very low
	9....(N.R.)	9....(N.R.)	9....(N.R.)
	5..neither(vol.)	5..neither(vol.)	5..neither(vol.)
THRIFT	(47)	(48)	(49)
	1....Very high	1....Very high	1....Very high
	2....High	2....High	2....High
	3....Low	3....Low	3....Low
	4....Very low	4....Very low	4....Very low
	9....(N.R.)	9....(N.R.)	9....(N.R.)
	5..neither(vol.)	5..neither(vol.)	5..neither(vol.)
INTEL-LIGENCE	(50)	(51)	(52)
	1....Very high	1....Very high	1....Very high
	2....High	2....High	2....High
	3....Low	3....Low	3....Low
	4....Very low	4....Very low	4....Very low
	9....(N.R.)	9....(N.R.)	9....(N.R.)
	5..neither(vol.)	5..neither(vol.)	5..neither(vol.)

	(53)	(54)	(55)
HONESTY	1... Very high	1... Very high	1... Very high
	2... High	2... High	2... High
	3... Low	3... Low	3... Low
	4... Very low	4... Very low	4... Very low
	9... (N.R.)	9... (N.R.)	9... (N.R.)
	5. neither(vol.)	5. neither(vol.)	5. neither(vol.)

	(56)	(57)	(58)
CLEANLI- NESS	1... Very high	1... Very high	1... Very high
	2... High	2... High	2... High
	3... Low	3... Low	3... Low
	4... Very low	4... Very low	4... Very low
	9... (N.R.)	9... (N.R.)	9... (N.R.)
	5. neither(vol.)	5. neither(vol.)	5. neither(vol.)

Vol. = Volunteered

12. I am going to describe some situations to you and I want to know your own reactions.

(a) Would you like it or not if you were eating at the same restaurant as (READ OUT IN TURN)

	Yes	No	Other Comments	N.R.	
an average Chinese	1	2	....	9	(59)
an average Malay	1	2	....	9	(60)
an average Indian	1	2	....	9	(61)

(b) Would you like it or not if you had to work with (READ OUT IN TURN)

	Yes	No	Other Comments	N.R.	
an average Chinese	1	2	....	9	(62)
an average Malay	1	2	....	9	(63)
an average Indian	1	2	....	9	(64)

(c) Would you like it or not if .... (READ OUT IN TURN) belonged to the same clubs and organisations as you?

	Yes	No	Other Comments	N.R.	
an average Chinese	1	2	....	9	(65)
an average Malay	1	2	....	9	(66)
an average Indian	1	2	....	9	(67)

(d) Would you like it or not if your neighbor was (READ OUT IN TURN)

	Yes	No	Other Comments	N.R.	
an average Chinese	1	2	....	9	(68)
an average Malay	1	2	....	9	(69)
an average Indian	1	2	....	9	(70)

(e) Would you like it or not if somebody from your own family married (READ OUT IN TURN)

	Yes	No	Other Comments	N.R.	
an average Chinese	1	2	....	9	(71)
an average Malay	1	2	....	9	(72)
an average Indian	1	2	....	9	(73)

Repeat Cols. 1–9	
CARD 2	(10)

SHOW CARD III (YELLOW)

13(a) Would you please tell me to what age-group you belong?

Up to 15 years	1	(11)
16–20 years	2	
21–25 years	3	
26–30 years	4	
31–35 years	5	
36–40 years	6	
41–50 years	7	
51–60 years	8	
61 and over	9	
(N.R.)	0	

(b) Would you please tell me what town you were born in? (ASK FOR STATE AND/OR COUNTRY IF NOT SURE)

Town ....

State ....

    1 2 3 4 5 6 7 8 9 0 x y   (12)
    1 2 3 4 5 6 7 8 9 0 x y   (13)

Country ....

(c) Could you please tell me what your religion is?

Muslim	1	(14)
Buddhist	2	
Taoist	3	
Other Chinese	**4**	
Hindu	5	
Other Indian	6	
Catholic	7	
Other Christian	8	
Others (write in)		

....

Not stated/No religion	9	

(c.1) Are you practising or not practising? (IF YES) Actively or occasionally?

Practising actively	1	(15)
Practising occasionally	2	
Non-practising	3	
(N.R.)	9	

(d) Could you please tell me your occupation?

....
....

1 2 3 4 5 6 7 8 9 0 x y	(16)
1 2 3 4 5 6 7 8 9 0 x y	(17)

14(a) Could you please tell me how many persons there are in your household? That is, how many people sleep here and *eat at the same table with you.*

1 2 3 4 5 6 7 8 9	(18)
If more than 9, write here	

14(b) How many persons are aged 15 and *below?*

0 1 2 3 4 5 6 7 8 9	(19)

(c) How many persons are aged *over* 15?

0 1 2 3 4 5 6 7 8 9

SHOW CARD III (YELLOW)

(d) Could you please tell me the ages of the persons aged *over* 15?

How many persons are there aged 16–20?
(ASK FOR EACH AGE GROUP)

16–20	1 2 3 4 5 6 7 8 9 0 x y	(20)
21–25	1 2 3 4 5 6 7 8 9 0 x y	**(21)**
26–30	1 2 3 4 5 6 7 8 9 0 x y	**(22)**
31–35	1 2 3 4 5 6 7 8 9 0 x y	**(23)**
36–40	1 2 3 4 5 6 7 8 9 0 x y	**(24)**
41–50	1 2 3 4 5 6 7 8 9 0 x y	**(25)**
51–60	1 2 3 4 5 6 7 8 9 0 x y	**(26)**
61 and over	1 2 3 4 5 6 7 8 9 0 x y	**(27)**

(e) Could you please tell me at what level you finished your education?

No schooling   1
_____   (28)
Went to school but did not complete primary   2
Completed primary (6 years)   3
_____
Secondary school 1–3 years   4
Chinese—Junior Middle 1–3 years
Malay—1–3 years
_____
Passed Form IV or Junior Cambridge   5
Chinese—Did *not* complete Senior Middle
Malay—Did not pass Senior Cambridge
_____
Passed Form V or Senior Cambridge   6
Chinese—Completed Senior Middle
Malay—Passed Senior Cambridge
_____
Completed H.S.C./College diploma after
    Senior Cambridge   7
University degree   8
Other (write in) . . . .
. . . .

(f) Would you please tell me what race you are?

Malay	1
Chinese	2
Indian	3
Ceylonese	4
Eurasian	5
Others (write in)	

. . . .
(N.R.)   9

(29) appears to the right of the race list.

(g) Would you please tell me what race your mother is? Your father? (RECORD EVEN IF DECEASED)

	Mother (30)	Father (31)
Malay	1	1
Chinese	2	2
Indian	3	3
Ceylonese	4	4
Eurasian	5	5
Others (write in)		
(N.R.)	9	9

14(h) Would you please tell me your marital status? Are you (READ OUT)

Single	1	(32)
Married	2	
Widowed	3	
Divorced	4	
Separated	5	
(N.R.)	9	

IF MARRIED
(h.1) Would you please tell me what race your wife/husband is?

Malay	1	(33)
Chinese	2	
Indian	3	
Eurasian	4	
Ceylonese	5	
Others (write in)		
(N.R.)	9	

RECORD SEX

Male	1	(34)
Female	2	

15(a) What other languages can you speak besides . . . . (language of interview)
(b) Which of these languages can you read and write in?
(c) What language did you grow up speaking in your house?

	(a)		(b)		(c)	
	Lang. of interview		Other langs. spoken		Langs. can read and write		Grow up speaking
Malay	1	(35)	1	(36)	1	(47)	1	(53)
Cantonese	2		1	(37)	–		1	(54)
Hokkien	3		1	(38)	–		1	(55)
Hakka	4		1	(39)	–		1	(56)
Teochew	5		1	(40)	–		1	(57)
Hainanese	6		1	(41)	–		1	(58)
Mandarin	7		1	(42)	1	(48)	1	(59)
Tamil	8		1	(43)	1	(49)	1	(60)
English	0		1	(44)	1	(50)	1	(61)
Others	. . . . . .		. . . . (45)		. . . . (51)		. . . . (62)
. . . .			. . . . (46)		. . . . (52)		. . . . (63)
(N.R.)			9		9		9

OFFICE USE ONLY	
No. of languages spoken	(64)
No. of languages read & written	(65)

16. In your opinion what are the most important political problems facing Malaysia today? (Probe: What else?) AT LEAST ONE AND UP TO THREE

. . . .
. . . .
. . . .

1 2 3 4 5 6 7 8 9 0 x y   (66)
1 2 3 4 5 6 7 8 9 0 x y   (67)
1 2 3 4 5 6 7 8 9 0 x y   (68)

One problem stated   1   (69)
Two problems stated   2
Three problems stated   3
N.R.   9

17(a) Are you registered to vote or not?

Yes   1
No   2 (GO TO Q. 18) (70)
N.R.   9

IF YES

(b) Have you voted in any election in the last 3 years?

Yes	1	(71)
No	2	
N.R.	9	

18(a) Are you a member of any political party or not?

Yes	1 (GO TO 18(b))	(72)
No	2 (GO TO 18(c))	
N.R.	9	

IF YES

(b) Which party?

1 2 3 4 5 6 7 8 9 0 x y   (73)

IF NO

(c) Which party do you think would do the best job in government?

1 2 3 4 5 6 7 8 9 0 x y   (74)

19(a) Are you interested in any form of sport or games or not?

Yes	1	
No	2	(END INTERVIEW)

IF YES

(b) Which sport are you most interested in?

. . . .
. . . .

"I hereby certify that this interview has been conducted honestly and to the best of my ability."

Time interview ended: _____

Interviewer No: 0 1 2 3 4 5 6 7 8 9   (75–76)

0 1 2 3 4 5 6 7 8 9

Interviewer's
Signature: _____

Date: _____

0 1 2 3 4 5 6 7 8 9   (77–78)
0 1 2 3 4 5 6 7 8 9

Appendix 2

Malayan Politics: A Review

Those who find the treatment of Malayan politics in chapter 3 restrictive or too brief may be interested in several comprehensive accounts of Malayan politics already published.

Three books make up the starting point for any interested student of Malayan politics. The first of these, K. J. Ratnam's *Communalism and the Political Process in Malaya*,[1] asserts the primacy of race in Malayan politics: "What is of direct concern here are the divisions which exist between the different communities, and which make communalism the most significant factor in the country's political process." [2] Ratnam reviews the history of constitutional government in Malaya, examines the issues of citizenship, the special position of the Malays, religion and language in Malaya, and explores party politics for the 1955 and 1959 general elections.

The second general treatment is R. S. Milne's *Government and Politics in Malaysia*.[3] Confirming Ratnam's view, Milne writes:

> More than anything else, the racial composition is the key to understanding the whole picture. It dictates the pattern of the economy, has helped to shape the Constitution, and has influenced the democratic process and the party system.[4]

Milne's treatment is in standard textual form. It contains a brief introductory history followed by chapters on federal-state relations, parties, elections and interest groups, the Parliament and state legislatures, the executive, the civil service, the judiciary, foreign policy, and Singapore, concluding with an evaluation of the prospects for national unity. Both of these writers are cautiously optimistic about the future of democratic politics in Malaya. Ratnam hoped that communal elements might be eradicated from politics, noting that the Alliance had institutionalized some measure of unity in its intercommunal partnership. Milne looked to this same leadership as the basis for his optimistic prognosis.

The third, and most complete, of the general treatments is Gordon P. Means' *Malaysian Politics*.[5] With the exception of an analytical concluding chapter, this book is a detailed month-by-month, at times day-by-day, account of important historical developments in Malaya, especially since World War II. Means' prognosis for Malaya's future is somewhat uncertain. In his final chapter, "An Interpretation of Malaysian Politics," he hedges the future, suggesting, on the one hand, that increased modernization might defuse the racial cleavage and, on the other hand, that the processes of politics are leading to even more pronounced racial tensions.

Issues, parties, and bureaucracies are the subject of another set of studies. In *Multi-Ethnic Politics: The Case of Malaysia,* Cynthia H. Enloe documents the emergence of the language issue in education policy.[6] Her study asserts that the actual process of policy formation has motivated racial integration. A policy that so directly affects each of the major races had the effect of inducing some form of interaction, even if it was conflictual at the outset. She ascribes to government the potential for shaping interracial patterns, rather than being simply a passive object of given racial conditions.

The most thorough account of political parties in Malaya (excluding the Alliance) is found in R. K. Vasil's *Politics in a Plural Society: A Study of Non-Communal Political Parties in West Malaysia*.[7] Vasil's thesis, based on primary material, unpublished party documents, and personal interviews, is that in the course of time each of the genuinely noncommunal political parties became converted into non-Malay parties and finally into non-Malay communal organizations. For Vasil, the failure of the noncommunal parties to retain a multiracial membership and outlook casts doubt on the viability of the political system and the possibility for integration among the different racial groups, especially since the Tunku is no longer able to compromise and moderate the demands of the different communities. The history of each party Vasil presents thus confirms my own conception of Malayan politics—that outbidding on the racial question meant the end of moderation and the failure of multiracialism in party organization.

Bureaucracy has been the subject of two books. The first is Robert O. Tilman's *Bureaucratic Transition in Malaya,* which explores the transition in the bureaucracy from chiefly expatriate to Malayan between 1957 and 1962.[8] Tilman concludes that non-Malays have done better than might be expected and that the bureaucracy, unlike that of many of Malaya's Asian neighbors, did not suffer a total collapse in administrative standards and efficiency.

Gayl D. Ness concentrates more intensively on the Ministry of Rural Development in *Bureaucracy and Rural Development in Malaysia.*[9] Ness credits the success of the rural development program to the superhuman efforts of Tun Abdul Razak, former deputy prime minister and now current prime minister of Malaya, who was able to force the bureaucracy to act effectively.

In addition to these books, many other articles and books analyze the results of each of Malaya's elections. Ratnam's book, cited earlier, covers the 1955 Legislative Council election and the 1959 general parliamentary election. A treatment of the 1964 election is found in Ratnam and Milne's *The Malayan Parliamentary Election of 1964.*[10] The only full length study of the most recent election is R. K. Vasil's *The Malaysian General Election of 1969.*[11]

More succinct treatments of the Malayan elections have appeared in periodicals. Francis G. Carnell and Irene Tinker provide accounts of the 1955 Legislative Council elections;[12] T. G. McGee, the 1959 parliamentary and State Legislative Assembly elections;[13] R. K. Vasil, the 1964 parliamentary and State Legislative Assembly elections;[14] and there are at least six separate treatments of the 1969 general elections in print: Ratnam and Milne, Martin Rudner, Jerome R. Bass, Stuart Drummond and David Hawkins, Nancy L. Snider, and Judith Goldman.[15] These election analyses confirm the steadily increasing importance of the racial issue and the Alliance's failure in 1969 to retain its unrivaled position.

Appendix 3

Registration of Societies

The ability to restrict or control social organization in the plural society may be used to mobilize members of specific races for political support. In Malaya, Malay social organizations receive official encouragement; the Chinese, on the other hand, suffer discouragements and perhaps outright bans on their voluntary organizations.

The cause and effect problem is not here easily resolvable. An analysis of the two tables in this appendix suggests that the Office of the Registrar of Societies has been active during the postindependence period of Malay rule. But the tables may also be interpreted to mean that Malays entered the postindependence period as a more rural, less organized community than the Chinese. Consequently, the numbers would reflect natural, rather than governmentally-induced artificial, processes. Probably some combination of the two is the correct explanation, but a better understanding awaits more thorough study.

In 1959, just two years after independence, the number of registered Chinese societies was approximately two-and-one-half times the number of registered Malay societies. By 1964 the numbers were about equal. Since then, Malay societies have grown at an absolutely greater rate. Even more interesting are the individual membership figures. The number of Chinese who belonged to lawfully registered societies in 1959 was fivefold that of Malays. (The number of multiracial societies and their membership has always been small in relation to the specifically racial organizations). By 1968 the numbers were about the same. This means that more than 800,000 Chinese who had belonged to lawfully registered societies in 1961 were no longer members by 1967, whereas (with the exception of 1967) Malay social membership grew steadily.

Table 20   REGISTERED SOCIETIES AND THEIR
MEMBERSHIPS BY RACE, 1959–1970

Year	Number of Chinese Societies	Membership in Chinese Societies	Number of Malay Societies	Membership in Malay Societies
1959	2,041	985,726	862	190,509
1960	2,094	1,083,838	1,111	191,699
1961	2,130	1,211,370	1,309	212,050
1962	2,141	885,684	1,576	220,524
1963	2,173	879,389	1,775	226,709
1964	2,228	828,495	2,299	298,459
1965	2,259	789,120	2,481	305,366
1966	2,457	—a	2,662	—
1967	2,881	360,969	2,953	288,509
1968	3,069	369,448	3,118	330,799
1969	3,156	—	3,326	—
1970	3,227	—	3,553	—
1971b	3,271	—	3,578	—

Sources: Annual Reports of the Registrar of Societies.
Notes: aThat these data are unavailable does not appear traceable to political reasons. The author was officially told that many lower-ranking civil servants had not bothered to compile these totals out of laziness.
b The 1971 totals are based on third-quarter statistics. Fourth-quarter totals are presented for the remaining years.

The Office of the Registrar of Societies also compiles and publishes information on the number and membership (when it is counted) of societies that are dissolved each year. The membership statistics are by far the more interesting in this table; it is clear that the cancellation of a Chinese society entails a more significant reduction in the number of Chinese involved than is true for Malay societies.

If the information contained in these tables is accurate, voluntary organization has grown substantially among Malays and has declined among Chinese.

Table 21 DISSOLVED SOCIETIES AND THEIR MEMBERSHIPS BY RACE, 1959–1970

Year	Number of Chinese Societies	Membership in Chinese Societies	Number of Malay Societies	Membership in Malay Societies
1959	426	127,907	176	30,974
1960	465	135,348	216	31,231
1961	499	142,268	267	35,066
1962	553	209,235	359	42,856
1963	573	211,888	442	46,325
1964	602	214,059	494	47,704
1965	634	218,450	613	54,478
1966	778	—[a]	873	—
1967	808	180,486	1,036	21,241
1968	832	180,756	1,183	22,093
1969	876	—	1,466	—
1970	931	—	1,622	—
1971[b]	974	—	1,900	—

Sources: Annual Reports of the Registrar of Societies.

Notes: [a] These data are unavailable.
[b] The 1971 totals are based on third-quarter statistics.

Appendix 4

The Transactions Hypothesis

The data in chapter 4 have been used to test a series of hypotheses collectively known as the "transactions model." * The chief hypothesis of this model is that the higher the rates of interaction among persons of different backgrounds, the greater their degree of integration. Since the word "integration" generally refers to feelings of cohesiveness among people, it is a difficult concept on which to pin any direct statistical measure.

Using the same questions that appeared in chapter 4 as different measures of the concept of "integration," I tried to test the transactions hypothesis. I found that higher rates of interracial social interaction led to higher levels of positive effect. Put more simply, people who deal with one another tend to like each other more than those who keep entirely to themselves. In a sense, then, the survey data supported the transaction hypothesis.

It was nevertheless disturbing that the survey data revealed increasingly higher levels of integration in Malaya as more of the population became educated. As this did not correspond to the obviously deteriorating political situation, I concluded that social effect ("integration") and democratic political stability were not

* See Alvin Rabushka, "Integration in Urban Malaya: Ethnic Attitudes among Malays and Chinese," *Journal of Asian and African Studies* 6, no. 2 (April 1971):91–107. In somewhat simplified form, the same transactions model was tested on a sample of University of Malaya students. See Alvin Rabushka, "Integration in a Multi-Racial Institution: Ethnic Attitudes among Chinese and Malay Students at the University of Malaya," *Race* 11, no. 1 (July 1969):53–63.

necessarily correlates. The transactions model, in retrospect, does not clearly distinguish the political and nonpolitical aspects of "integration."

Though the reader is invited to study the footnoted article, its major results are summarized as follows.

1. Living in a multiracial neighborhood increased affect ("integration") only when social interaction increased. Curiously, those people who lived in the multiracial parts of Kuala Lumpur and Penang and stayed chiefly among their own kind had lower social distance (tolerance) scores than the residents of racial ghettoes.

2. Persons with more education were significantly more integrated with members of other races than those with little or no education—an obvious policy prescription. Nearly all the better educated, however, are products of the English schools, and the government's decision to gradually abolish the English schools may not produce increased racial harmony.

3. Age, religious, and sexual differences have little impact on the extent of racial integration.

Notes

1: INTRODUCTION

1. See Alvin Rabushka and Kenneth A. Shepsle, *Politics in Plural Societies: A Theory of Democratic Instability* (Columbus, Ohio: Charles E. Merrill, 1972).

2. K. J. Ratnam, *Communalism and the Political Process in Malaya* (Kuala Lumpur: University of Malaya Press, 1965), pp. v–vi.

3. K. J. Ratnam and R. S. Milne, *The Malayan Parliamentary Election of 1964* (Singapore: University of Malaya Press, 1967), p. 3.

4. Gayl D. Ness, *Bureaucracy and Rural Development in Malaysia* (Berkeley and Los Angeles: University of California Press, 1967), p. 69.

5. Ibid., p. x.

6. Robert O. Tilman, *Pacific Affairs* 42, no. 4 (winter 1969–70):535.

7. Richard Rose, *Governing Without Consent: An Irish Perspective* (Boston: Beacon, 1971).

8. See, for instance, a recently published book on Malaya by R. K. Vasil, *Politics in a Plural Society: A Study of Non-Communal Political Parties in West Malaysia* (Kuala Lumpur and Singapore: Oxford University Press for the Australian Institute of International Affairs, 1971).

9. J. S. Furnivall, *Netherlands India* (Cambridge: Cambridge University Press, 1939), p. 446.

10. See, for example, H. S. Morris, "Indians in East Africa: A Study in a Plural Society," *British Journal of Sociology* 7, no. 3

(October 1953):194–211; Burton Benedict, "Stratification in Plural Societies," *American Anthropologist* 64, no. 6 (December 1962):1235–46; Daniel Crowley, "Plural and Differential Acculturation in Trinidad," *American Anthropologist* 59, no. 5 (October 1957):817–24; and Lloyd Braithwaite, "The Problem of Cultural Integration in Trinidad," *Social and Economic Studies* 3, no. 1 (June 1954):82–96.

11. A selection of the various treatments may be found in M. G. Smith, *The Plural Society in the British West Indies* (Berkeley and Los Angeles: University of California Press, 1965); Leo A. Despres, *Cultural Pluralism and Nationalist Politics in British Guiana* (Chicago: Rand McNally & Co., 1967); and Pierre L. van den Berghe, *Race and Racism: A Comparative Perspective* (New York: John Wiley, 1967). This selection is not exhaustive, but it does provide a sample of the different views on the prospects for plural societies.

12. Primary examples include Amitai Etzioni, *Political Unification: A Comparative Study of Leaders and Forces* (New York: Holt, Rinehart & Winston, 1965); Karl W. Deutsch et al., *Political Community and the North Atlantic Area: International Organization in the Light of Historical Experience* (Princeton: Princeton University Press, 1957); Philip E. Jacob and Henry Teune, "The Integrative Process: Guidelines for the Analysis of the Bases of Political Community," in Philip E. Jacob and James V. Toscano, eds., *The Integration of Political Communities* (Philadelphia: Lippincott, 1964); Seymour Martin Lipset, *Political Man: The Social Bases of Politics* (Garden City, New York: Anchor Books, 1963); Leonard Binder, "National Integration and Political Development," *American Political Science Review* 58, no. 3 (September 1964):622–32; and Arend Lijphart, *The Politics of Accommodation: Pluralism and Democracy in the Netherlands* (Berkeley and Los Angeles: University of California Press, 1968).

13. Rabushka and Shepsle, *Politics in Plural Societies,* chap. 1.

2: CULTURAL AND POLITICAL SETTING

1. See Paul Wheatley, *The Golden Khersonese* (London: Oxford University Press, 1962).

2. Histories of Malaya are plentiful. The following are suggested for the interested reader: Harry Miller, *The Story of Malaysia* (London: Faber & Faber, 1965); K. G. Tregonning, *A History of Modern Malaya* (Singapore: Eastern Universities Press, 1964); Joginder Singh Jessy, *History of Malaya (1400–1959)* (Penang: United Publishers and Peninsular Publications, 1961); G. P. Dartford, *A Short History of Malaya* (Kuala Lumpur: Longmans of Malaya, 1958); N. J. Ryan, *The Making of Modern Malaya* (Kuala Lumpur: Oxford University Press, 1965); J. Kennedy, *A History of Malaya* (London: Macmillan & Co., 1962); R. O. Winstedt, *A History of Malaya* (Singapore: Marican & Sons, 1962); Victor Purcell, *Malaysia* (New York: Walker & Co., 1965); Norton Ginsburg and Chester F. Roberts, Jr., *Malaya* (Seattle: University of Washington Press, 1958); R. N. Jackson, *Immigrant Labor and the Development of Malaya, 1786–1920* (Federation of Malaya: Government Press, 1961); J. Norman Parmer, "Part Four: Malaysia," in George McT. Kahin, ed., *Government and Politics in Southeast Asia* (Ithaca: Cornell University Press, 1964); F. J. Moorhead, *A History of Malaya, Volume One and Volume Two* (Kuala Lumpur: Longmans of Malaya, 1963); J. M. Gullick, *Malaya* (London: Ernest Benn, 1964); and Kernial Singh Sandhu, *Indians in Malaya: Some Aspects of their Immigration and Settlement (1786–1957)* (Cambridge: Cambridge University Press, 1969).

3. For Malay magic, customs, traditions, etc., see Walter W. Skeat, *Malay Magic* (New York: Dover Publications, 1967); R. O. Winstedt, *The Malays: A Cultural History,* 3rd ed. rev. (London: Routledge & Kegan Paul, 1953); and Michael K. Endicott, *An Analysis of Malay Magic* (London: Oxford University Press, 1970).

4. See Martin Rudner, "The State and Peasant Innovation in Rural Development: The Case of Malaysian Rubber," *Asian and African Studies* (Annual of the Israel Oriental Society), vol. 6 (1970):75–96.

5. *Straits Times,* 17 July 1971, p. 22.

6. Federation of Malaya. *Annual Report of the Trade Unions Registry for the Years 1957, 1960, 1962, 1964* (Kuala Lumpur: Government Press).

7. Major studies about trade unions include: Charles Gamba, *The Origins of Trade Unionism in Malaya* (Singapore: Eastern Universities Press, 1962); Alex Josey, *Trade Unionism in Malaya* (Singapore: Donald Moore, 1954); Michael R. Stenson, *Industrial Conflict in Malaya* (Kuala Lumpur: Oxford University Press, 1970); and Martin Rudner, "Malayan Labor in Transition: Labor Policy and Trade Unionism, 1955–1963," *Modern Asian Studies,* in press.

8. *Household Budget Survey,* Report of Inland Revenue Department, 1958, cited in T. H. Silcock, "Communal and Party Structure," in T. H. Silcock and E. K. Fisk, eds., *The Political Economy of Independent Malaya* (Canberra: Australian National University Press, 1963), p. 3. The *Household Budget Survey* probably underestimates the "real income" of Malays. Rural Malays directly consume a portion of their own output which does not, therefore, enter into "money income" calculations.

9. Alvin Rabushka, "Intermarrriage in Malaya: Some Notes on the Persistence of the Race Factor," *Asia Quarterly* (1971/1):103–108.

10. Excellent treatments of this subject may be found in Harry E. Groves, *The Constitution of Malaysia* (Singapore: Malaysia Publications, 1964) and L. A. Sheridan and Harry E. Groves, *The Constitution of Malaysia* (Dobbs Ferry, New York: Oceana Publications, 1967).

11. For a full account, see James De V. Allen, *The Malayan Union,* Monograph Series, no. 10 (New Haven: Yale Southeast Asia Studies, 1967).

12. C. T. Edwards, *Public Finances in Malaya and Singapore* (Canberra: Australian National University Press, 1970), p. 32.

13. For an analysis of the language issue in Malayan politics, see Cynthia H. Enloe, *Multi-Ethnic Politics: The Case of Malaysia,* Research Monograph, no. 2 (Berkeley: Center for South and Southeast Asia Studies, 1970).

14. See R. K. Vasil, *Politics in a Plural Society: A Study of Non-Communal Political Parties in West Malaysia* (Kuala Lumpur and Singapore: Oxford University Press for the Australian Institute of International Affairs, 1971), chap. 8.

15. K. J. Ratnam and R. S. Milne, "The 1969 Parliamentary

Election in West Malaysia," *Pacific Affairs* 43, no. 2 (summer 1970):220.

16. *Straits Times,* 18 July 1971, p. 1; 31 July 1971, p. 1; and 1 August 1971, p. 6.

17. Only those features of each city that are relevant to this study are discussed. For more details about Kuala Lumpur, see T. G. McGee, "The Cultural Role of Cities: A Case Study of Kuala Lumpur," *Journal of Tropical Geography* 17 (May 1963):178–96; W. J. Bennett, "Kuala Lumpur: A Town of the Equatorial Lowlands," *Tijdschrift voor economische en sociale geografie* (December 1961):327–33; Pao-Chun Tsou, *Urban Landscape of Kuala Lumpur: A Geographical Survey* (Singapore: Institute of Southeast Asia, Nanyang University, 1967); J. M. Gullick, *The Story of Early Kuala Lumpur* (Singapore: Donald Moore, 1956); and Federation of Malaya, *Kuala Lumpur 100 Years* (Kuala Lumpur: Kuala Lumpur Municipal Council, 1959). For more information about Penang see: W. D. McTaggart, *Social Survey of Penang* (George Town: City Council of George Town, Penang, 1966) and *Penang Past and Present 1786–1963: A Historical Account of the City of George Town since 1786* (George Town: City Council of George Town, Penang, 1966).

18. Federation of Malaya, *Inventory of Squatter Housing Types, Households and Population* (Kuala Lumpur: Commissioner of the Federal Capital of Kuala Lumpur, 1964).

19. Tsou, *Urban Landscape of Kuala Lumpur,* p. 29.

3: AN OVERVIEW OF MALAYAN POLITICS

1. This assumption can be formally represented and its implications for both cooperative and conflictual behavior logically drawn out. For the logical demonstration that relies upon a mathematical treatment of intensity and uncertainty, see Alvin Rabushka and Kenneth A. Shepsle, *Politics in Plural Societies,* chaps. 2 and 3.

2. Gordon P. Means, *Malaysian Politics* (New York: New York University Press, 1970), p. 165.

3. For details of the riots and their implications, see Felix V. Gagliano, *Communal Violence in Malaysia 1969: The Political*

Aftermath, Southeast Asia Series, no. 13, (Athens, Ohio: 1970); Mahathir bin Mohamad, *The Malay Dilemma* (Singapore: Donald Moore, 1970); and John Slimming, *Malaysia, Death of a Democracy* (London: John Murray, 1969).

4. C. T. Edwards, *Public Finances in Malaya and Singapore.*

5. Ibid., p. 78.

6. Ibid., p. 89.

7. Ibid., p. 81.

8. Ibid., p. 344.

9. Ibid., p. 30.

4: INTERRACIAL VALUES AND SOCIAL BEHAVIOR

1. "Communal and Party Structure," in T. H. Silcock and E. K. Fisk, eds., *The Political Economy of Independent Malaya,* p. 5.

2. Gayl D. Ness, *Bureaucracy and Rural Development in Malaysia,* p. 46.

3. *Stories and Sketches by Sir Frank Swettenham.* Selected and introduced by William R. Roff (Kuala Lumpur: Oxford University Press, 1967), pp. 16–17.

4. Peter J. Wilson, *A Malay Village and Malaysia* (New Haven: Human Relations Area Files, 1967), pp. 25, 30–31.

5. Tjoa Soei Hock, *Institutional Background to Modern Economic and Social Development in Malaya* (Kuala Lumpur: Liu & Liu Agency, 1963), pp. 3–15.

6. Victor Purcell, *Malaysia,* pp. 42–43, 47.

7. The implications of an uneven admixture of Malays and Chinese in the larger urban areas are explored in Anthony Reid, "The Kuala Lumpur Riots and the Malaysian Political System," *Australian Outlook* 23, no. 3 (1969):258–78.

5: RACIAL POLITICS IN MICROCOSM

1. A discussion of Malayan local government is found in R. S. Milne, *Government and Politics in Malaysia* (Boston: Houghton Mifflin, 1967), chap. 10.

2. Federation of Malaya, *Report on the Introduction of Elections in the Municipality of George Town, Penang, 1951* (Kuala Lumpur: Government Press, 1953).

3. Federation of Malaya, *The Local Authorities Election Ordinance, 1950.*

4. "Communal and Party Structure," in T. H. Silcock and E. K. Fisk, eds., *The Political Economy of Independent Malaya,* pp. 20–21. The 1962 elections were, however, confined to councils of former new villages; hence, the 1961 elections should be accorded greater significance. For an analysis of the 1961 local elections that concentrates on party rather than on racial success, see T. E. Smith, "The Local Authority Elections 1961 in the Federation of Malaya," *Journal of Commonwealth Political Studies* 1, no. 2 (March 1962):153–55.

5. *Sunday Times,* 1 August 1965.

6. *Straits Times,* 31 January 1969, p. 15.

7. Ibid., 8 July 1971, p. 1.

8. Ibid., 14 July 1971, p. 9.

9. Malaysia, *Report of the Royal Commission of Enquiry to Investigate into the Workings of Local Authorities in West Malaysia* (Kuala Lumpur: Government Press, 1970, Dated December 1968).

10. *Straits Times,* 11 December 1971, p. 17.

11. T. E. Smith, *Report on the First Election of Members to the Legislative Council* (Kuala Lumpur: Government Press, 1955), p. 10; *Straits Times,* 19 August 1959.

12. For a detailed account of one Kuala Lumpur race in the 1964 parliamentary election, see R. K. Vasil, "Batu (Selangor)," in K. J. Ratnam and R. S. Milne, *The Malayan Parliamentary Election of 1964*: pp. 242–65. Vasil tabulated the racial composition of the voters in Batu from an analysis of the electoral rolls. This data, combined with survey research in the constituency, would give a real picture of racial voting practices.

6: CONCLUSION

1. For an exception, see Lewis H. Gann and Peter Duignan, *White Settlers in Tropical Africa* (Baltimore: Penguin, 1962).

2. Two examples are Gary S. Becker, *The Economics of Discrimination,* 2nd ed. (Chicago: University of Chicago Press, 1971) and William H. Hutt, *The Economics of the Colour Bar* (London: A. Deutsch, 1964). Becker treats discrimination in a general theoretical sense, whereas Hutt presents a detailed analysis of South Africa.

3. Robert Kearney, *Communalism and Language in the Politics of Ceylon* (Durham, N.C.: Duke University Press, 1967), p. 15.

4. Ibid., p. 40.

5. Ivar Oxaal, *Black Intellectuals Come to Power* (Cambridge, Mass.: Schenkman Publishing Co., 1968).

6. Milton J. Esman, *Administration and Development in Malaysia: Institution Building and Reform in a Plural Society* (Ithaca and London: Cornell University Press, 1972), p. 55.

APPENDIX 2

1. K. J. Ratnam, *Communalism and the Political Process in Malaya.*

2. Ibid., p. 5.

3. R. S. Milne, *Government and Politics in Malaysia.*

4. Ibid., p. 3.

5. Gordon P. Means, *Malaysian Politics.*

6. Cynthia H. Enloe, *Multi-Ethnic Politics.*

7. R. K. Vasil, *Politics in a Plural Society.*

8. Robert O. Tilman, *Bureaucratic Transition in Malaya* (Durham, N.C.: Duke University Press, 1964).

9. Gayl D. Ness, *Bureaucracy and Rural Development in Malaysia.*

10. K. J. Ratnam and R. S. Milne, *The Malayan Parliamentary Election of 1964.*

11. R. K. Vasil, *The Malaysian General Election of 1969,* (Kuala Lumpur: Oxford University Press, 1972).

12. Francis G. Carnell, "The Malayan Elections," *Pacific Affairs* 28, no. 4 (December 1955): 315–30, and Irene Tinker, "Ma-

layan Elections: Electoral Pattern for Plural Societies?" *Western Political Quarterly* 9, no. 2 (June 1956):258–82.

13. T. G. McGee, "The Malayan Elections of 1959. A Study of Electoral Geography," *Journal of Tropical Geography* 16 (October 1962): 70–99.

14. R. K. Vasil, "The 1964 General Elections in Malaya," *International Studies* 7, no. 1 (July 1965): 20–65.

15. K. J. Ratnam and R. S. Milne, "The 1969 Parliamentary Election in West Malaysia," *Pacific Affairs* 43, no. 2 (summer 1970):203–26; Martin Rudner, "The Malaysian General Election of 1969: A Political Analysis," *Modern Asian Studies* 4, no. 1 (1970):1–21; Jerome R. Bass, "Malaysia: Continuity or Change?" *Asian Survey,* 10, no. 2 (February 1970):152–60; Stuart Drummond and David Hawkins, "The Malaysian Elections of 1969: An Analysis of the Campaign and the Results," *Asian Survey* 10, no. 4 (April 1970):320–35; Nancy L. Snider, "Race, Leitmotiv of the Malayan Election Drama," *Asian Survey* 10, no. 12 (December 1970):1070–80; and Judith Goldman, "Party Support in Western Malaysia: Results of the First Stage of an Ecological Inquiry," *Asian Survey* 11, no. 6 (June 1971):582–609. The 1959 and 1964 elections are also analyzed here.

Bibliography

BOOKS

Allen, James De V. *The Malayan Union*. Monograph Series, no. 10. New Haven: Yale Southeast Asia Studies, 1967.

Bock, John C. *Education and Nation-Building in Malaysia*. Princeton: Princeton University Press, 1972.

————. *The Educational Correlates of Violence: A Case Study of Malaysia*, forthcoming.

Dartford, G. P. *A Short History of Malaya*. Kuala Lumpur: Longmans of Malaya, 1958.

Edwards, C. T. *Public Finances in Malaya and Singapore*. Canberra: Australian National University Press, 1970.

Endicott, Michael K. *An Analysis of Malay Magic*. London: Oxford University Press, 1970.

Enloe, Cynthia H. *Multi-Ethnic Politics: The Case of Malaysia*. Monograph no. 2. Berkeley: Center for South and Southeast Asia Studies, 1970.

Esman, Milton J. *Administration and Development in Malaysia: Institution Building and Reform in a Plural Society*. Ithaca and London: Cornell University Press, 1972.

Furnivall, J. S. *Netherlands India*. Cambridge: Cambridge University Press, 1939.

Gagliano, Felix V. *Communal Violence in Malaysia 1969: The Political Aftermath*. Southeast Asia Series, no. 13. Athens, Ohio, 1970.

Gamba, Charles. *The Origins of Trade Unionism in Malaya*. Singapore: Eastern Universities Press, 1962.

136

Ginsburg, Norton and Roberts, Jr., Chester F. *Malaya*. Seattle: University of Washington Press, 1958.

Groves, Harry E. *The Constitution of Malaysia*. Singapore: Malaysia Publications, 1964.

Gullick, J. M. *Indigenous Political Systems of Western Malaya*. London: Athlone Press, 1958.

―――. *Malaya*. London: Ernest Benn, 1964.

―――. *The Story of Early Kuala Lumpur*. Singapore: Donald Moore, 1956.

Jackson, R. N. *Immigrant Labor and the Development of Malaya, 1786–1920*. Federation of Malaya: Government Press, 1961.

Jessy, Joginder Singh. *History of Malaya (1400–1959)*. Penang: United Publishers and Peninsular Publications, 1961.

Josey, Alex. *Trade Unionism in Malaya*. Singapore: Donald Moore, 1954.

Kennedy, J. *A History of Malaya*. London: Macmillan & Co., 1962.

Mahathir bin Mohamad. *The Malay Dilemma*. Singapore: Donald Moore, 1970.

McTaggart, W. D. *Social Survey of Penang*. George Town: City Council of George Town, Penang, 1966.

Means, Gordon P. *Malaysian Politics*. New York: New York University Press, 1970.

Miller, Harry. *The Story of Malaysia*. London: Faber and Faber, 1965.

Milne, R. S. *Government and Politics in Malaysia*. Boston: Houghton Mifflin, 1967.

Moorhead, F. J. *A History of Malaya, Volume One and Volume Two*. Kuala Lumpur: Longmans of Malaya, 1963.

Ness, Gayl D. *Bureaucracy and Rural Development in Malaysia*. Berkeley and Los Angeles: University of California Press, 1967.

Penang Past and Present 1786–1963: A Historical Account of the City of George Town since 1786. George Town: City Council of George Town, Penang, 1966.

Purcell, Victor. *Malaysia*. New York: Walker & Co., 1965.

Rabushka, Alvin and Shepsle, Kenneth A. *Politics in Plural Societies: A Theory of Democratic Instability.* Columbus, Ohio: Charles E. Merrill, 1972.

Ratnam, K. J. *Communalism and the Political Process in Malaya.* Kuala Lumpur: University of Malaya Press, 1965.

————and Milne, R. S. *The Malayan Parliamentary Election of 1964.* Singapore: University of Malaya Press, 1967.

Ryan, N. J. *The Making of Modern Malaya.* Kuala Lumpur: Oxford University Press, 1965.

Sandhu, Kernial Singh. *Indians in Malaya: Some Aspects of their Immigration and Settlement (1786–1957).* Cambridge: Cambridge University Press, 1969.

Sheridan, L. A. and Groves, Harry E. *The Constitution of Malaysia.* Dobbs Ferry, New York: Oceana Publications, 1967.

Silcock, T. H. and Fisk, E. K., eds. *The Political Economy of Independent Malaya.* Canberra: Australian National University Press, 1963.

Skeat, Walter W. *Malay Magic.* New York: Dover Publications, 1967.

Slimming, John. *Malaysia, Death of a Democracy.* London: John Murray, 1969.

Smith, T. E. *Report on the First Election of Members to the Legislative Council.* Kuala Lumpur: Government Press, 1955.

Stenson, Michael R. *Industrial Conflict in Malaya.* Kuala Lumpur: Oxford University Press, 1970.

Stories and Sketches by Sir Frank Swettenham. Selected and introduced by William R. Roff. Kuala Lumpur: Oxford University Press, 1967.

Tilman, Robert O. *Bureaucratic Transition in Malaya.* Durham, N.C.: Duke University Press, 1964.

Tjoa Soei Hock. *Institutional Background to Modern Economic and Social Development in Malaya.* Kuala Lumpur: Liu & Liu Agency, 1963.

Tregonning, K. G. *A History of Modern Malaya.* Singapore: Eastern Universities Press, 1964.

Tsou, Pao-chun. *Urban Landscape of Kuala Lumpur: A Geo-*

graphical Survey. Singapore: Institute of Southeast Asia, Nan-yang University, 1967.

Vasil, R. K. *Politics in a Plural Society: A Study of Non-Communal Political Parties in West Malaysia*. Kuala Lumpur and Singapore: Oxford University Press for the Australian Institute of International Affairs, 1971.

Wheatley, Paul. *The Golden Khersonese*. London: Oxford University Press, 1962.

Wilson, Peter J. *A Malay Village and Malaysia*. New Haven: Human Relations Area Files, 1967.

Winstedt, R. O. *A History of Malaya*. Singapore: Marican & Sons, 1962.

————. *The Malays: A Cultural History*. 3rd ed., rev. London: Routledge & Kegan Paul, 1953.

PERIODICALS

Bass, Jerome R., "Malaysia: Continuity or Change?" *Asian Survey* 10, no. 2 (February 1970):152–60.

Bennett, W. J. "Kuala Lumpur: A Town of the Equatorial Lowlands." *Tijdschrift voor economische en sociale geografie* (December 1961):327–33.

Carnell, Francis G. "The Malayan Elections." *Pacific Affairs* 28, no. 4 (December 1955):315–30.

Drummond, Stuart and Hawkins, David. "The Malaysian Elections of 1969: An Analysis of the Campaign and the Results." *Asian Survey* 10, no. 4 (April 1970):320–35.

Goldman, Judith. "Party Support in Western Malaysia: Results of the First Stage of an Ecological Inquiry." *Asian Survey* 11, no. 6 (June 1971):582–609.

Grossholtz, Jean. "Integrative Factors in the Malaysian and Phillipine Legislatures." *Comparative Politics* 3, no. 1 (October 1970):93–113.

McGee, T. G. "The Cultural Role of Cities: A Case Study of Kuala Lumpur." *Journal of Tropical Geography* 17 (May 1963):178–96.

————. "The Malayan Elections of 1959. A Study in Electoral Geography." *Journal of Tropical Geography* 16 (October 1962):70–99.

Rabushka, Alvin. "Affective, Cognitive and Behavioral Consistency of Chinese-Malay Interracial Attitudes." *Journal of Social Psychology* 82 (October 1970):35–41.

————. "A Note on Overseas Chinese Political Participation in Urban Malaya." *American Political Science Review* 64, no. 1 (March 1970):177–78.

————. "Integration in a Multi-Racial Institution: Ethnic Attitudes among Chinese and Malay Students at the University of Malaya." *Race* 11, no. 1 (July 1969):53–63.

————. "Integration in Urban Malaya: Ethnic Attitudes among Malays and Chinese." *Journal of Asian and African Studies* 6, no. 2 (April 1971):91–107.

————. "Intermarriage in Malaya: Some Notes on the Persistence of the Race Factor." *Asia Quarterly* (1971/1):103–108.

————. "Racial Stereotypes in Malaya." *Asian Survey* 11, no. 7 (July 1971):709–16.

————. "The Manipulation of Ethnic Politics in Malaya." *Polity* 2, no. 3 (spring 1970):345–56.

———— and Shepsle, Kenneth A. "Political Entrepreneurship and Patterns of Democratic Instability in Plural Societies." *Race* 12, no. 4 (April 1971):461–76.

Ratnam, K. J. and Milne, R. S. "The 1969 Parliamentary Election in West Malaysia." *Pacific Affairs* 43, no. 2 (summer 1970):203–26.

Reid, Anthony. "The Kuala Lumpur Riots and the Malaysian Political System." *Australian Outlook* 23, no. 3 (1969):258–78.

Rudner, Martin. "Malayan Labor in Transition: Labor Policy and Trade Unionism, 1955–1963." *Modern Asian Studies,* in press.

————. "The Malaysian General Election of 1969: A Political Analysis." *Modern Asian Studies* 4, no. 1 (1970):1–21.

————. "The State and Peasant Innovation in Rural Development: The Case of Malaysian Rubber." *Asian and African Studies* (Annual of the Israel Oriental Society), vol. 6 (1970):75–96.

Smith, T. E. "The Local Authority Elections 1961 in the Federation of Malaya." *Journal of Commonwealth Political Studies* 1, no. 2 (March 1962):153–55.

Snider, Nancy L. "Race, Leitmotiv of the Malayan Election Drama." *Asian Survey* 10, no. 12 (December 1970):1070–80.

Tinker, Irene. "Malayan Elections: Electoral Pattern for Plural Societies." *Western Political Quarterly* 9, no. 2 (June 1956):258–82.

Vasil, R. K. "The 1964 General Elections in Malaya." *International Studies* 7, no. 1 (July 1965):20–65.

OFFICIAL REPORTS

Federation of Malaya. *Annual Report of the Trade Unions Registry for the Years 1957, 1960, 1962, 1964*. Kuala Lumpur: Government Press.

————. *City Council of George Town, Penang. Reports,* 1957–63.

————. Election Commission. *Report on the Parliamentary (Dewan Ra'ayat) and State Legislative Assembly General Elections, 1964, of the States of Malaya*. Kuala Lumpur: Government Press, 1965.

————. Election Commission. *Report on the Parliamentary and State Elections, 1959*. Kuala Lumpur: Government Press, 1960.

————. *Federal Capital Act no. 35 of 1960*.

————. Fell, H. *1957 Population Census of the Federation of Malaya, Reports nos. 2, 3, 14*. Kuala Lumpur: Department of Statistics, 1957.

————. *Household Budget Survey*. Report of Inland Revenue Department, 1958.

————. *Inventory of Squatter Housing Types, Households and Population*. Kuala Lumpur: Commissioner of the Federal Capital of Kuala Lumpur, 1964.

————. *Kuala Lumpur Municipal Council Annual Reports,* 1954–61.

————. *Kuala Lumpur 100 Years*. Kuala Lumpur: Kuala Lumpur Municipal Council, 1959.

————. *The Local Authorities Election Ordinance, 1950.*

————. *The Local Councils Ordinance, 1952.*

————. *The Local Government Elections Act, 1960.*

————. *Monthly Statistical Bulletin.* Kuala Lumpur: Department of Statistics, 1966.

————. *Municipality of George Town, Penang, Reports, 1951–56.*

————. Penang State Government Gazette. *City Council of George Town (Transfer of Functions) Order, 1966.*

————. Penang State Government Gazette. *Local Authorities Elections (Penang) Order, 1959.*

————. Penang State Government Gazette. *Local Authorities Elections (Penang) Order, 1960.*

————. Penang State Government Gazette. *Municipal (Amendment) (Penang) Enactment, 1966.*

————. *Report on the Introduction of Elections in the Municipality of George Town, Penang, 1951.* Kuala Lumpur: Government Press, 1953.

————. Selangor State Government Gazette. *Local Authorities Elections (Selangor) Order, 1959.*

————. Selangor State Government Gazette. *Local Authorities Elections (Selangor) Order, 1960.*

Malaysia. Chander, R. *1970 Population and Housing Census of Malaysia, Community Groups.* Kuala Lumpur: Department of Statistics, 1972.

————. *Constitution (Amendment) Act, 1969.*

————. *Election Offences (Amendment) Act, 1969.*

————. *Report of the Royal Commission of Enquiry to Investigate into the Workings of Local Authorities in West Malaysia.* Kuala Lumpur: Government Press, 1970.

————. *Second Malaysia Plan, 1971–1975.* Kuala Lumpur: Government Press, 1971.

NEWSPAPERS

Straits Times.

Sunday Times.

Index

Abdul Aziz bin Ishak, 74
Aborigines, 16-17
Alliance Party, 36, 37, 48, 49, 50, 51, 52n; electoral performance of, 48, 50-51, 69, 74, 77, 79, 81, 93; origin of, 47; use of ambiguity, 48-50
Anglo-Dutch Treaty of 1824, 17
Athi Nahappan, 77, 78
Attitude scales, 56-67; cultural ethnocentrism, 59-60; racial behavior, 58-59; racial stereotypes, 63-67; social toleration, 61-63

Bock, John, 4n, 10
British East India Company, 27
British immigration policy, 17, 18
British resident advisers, 28
Buddhism, 26, 57

Cabinet, 30, 37, 51
Chin Peng, 52n
Chinese dynastic histories, 16
Chinese in Malaya, Malays' attitude to, 61-67; occupations of, 24; population distribution of, 20-22; racial stereotypes of, 64-67; religion of, 26, 57; urbanization of, 20, 22, 24; wealth of, 26
Choice, and individual preferences, 44-45; politics as, 43-45; and public decision rule, 43-44
Christianity, 26
Citizenship, 46; and effect on elections, 30, 82-83; of Malay and non Malays, 30, 49; restrictive requirements of, 32-33, 49, 69
Civil Rights, restriction of, 32
Colonialism, government and administration, 28-29, 72; policies of, 17-19, 27-29, 47
Communalism, 9n, 14, 34, 42, 54, 69
Communism in Malaya, 37
Confrontation of Malaya by Indonesia, 48, 75
Confucianism, 26
Constituency delimitation, and gerrymandering, 33, 83, 101
Constitution, and Federation of Malaya, 29; and guarantees for non-Malays, 31, 32, 101; important provisions of, 31-32

143

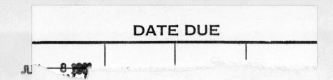

DATE DUE